EASY GUITAR

THE
CHRISTMAS CLASSICS
BOOK

ISBN 0-634-06248-4

HAL•LEONARD®
CORPORATION

7777 W. BLUEMOUND RD. P.O. BOX 13819 MILWAUKEE, WI 53213

For all works contained herein:
Unauthorized copying, arranging, adapting, recording or public performance is an infringement of copyright.
Infringers are liable under the law.

Visit Hal Leonard Online at
www.halleonard.com

THE CHRISTMAS CLASSICS BOOK

STRUM AND PICK PATTERNS

This chart contains the suggested strum and pick patterns that are referred to by number at the beginning
of each song in this book. The symbols ⊓ and ∨ in the strum patterns refer to down and up strokes, respectively.
The letters in the pick patterns indicate which right-hand fingers plays which strings.

p = thumb
i = index finger
m = middle finger
a = ring finger

For example; Pick Pattern 2
is played: thumb - index - middle - ring

Strum Patterns

Pick Patterns

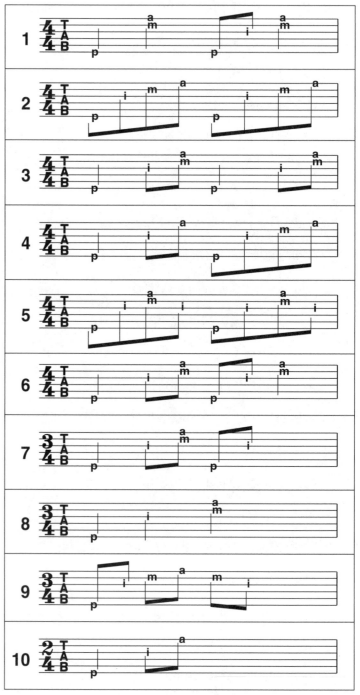

You can use the 3/4 Strum or Pick Patterns in songs written in compound meter (6/8, 9/8, 12/8, etc.).
For example, you can accompany a song in 6/8 by playing the 3/4 pattern twice in each measure.
The 4/4 Strum and Pick Patterns can be used for songs written in cut time (¢) by doubling the note
time values in the patterns. Each pattern would therefore last two measures in cut time.

Blue Holiday

Words and Music by Luther Dixon and Willie Denson

Strum Pattern: 4
Pick Pattern: 1

© 1961 (Renewed 1989) EMI LONGITUDE MUSIC and KILYNN MUSIC PUBLISHING INC.
All Rights Reserved   International Copyright Secured   Used by Permission

As Long as There's Christmas

from Walt Disney's BEAUTY AND THE BEAST - THE ENCHANTED CHRISTMAS

Music by Rachel Portman
Lyrics by Don Black

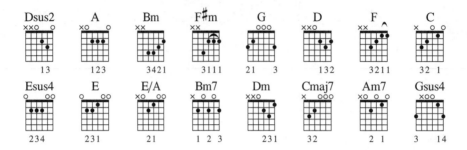

Strum Pattern: 7, 8
Pick Pattern: 7, 8

Intro
Moderately slow

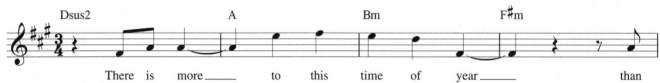

There is more ___ to this time of year ___ than

sleigh_ bells ___ and hol - ly, mis - tle - toe and snow. Those things will come and

Verse
A tempo

go. 1. Don't look in - side ___ a stock - ing. Don't look

un - der ___ the tree. The one thing we're_ look - ing for ___ is some - thing we can't_ see..

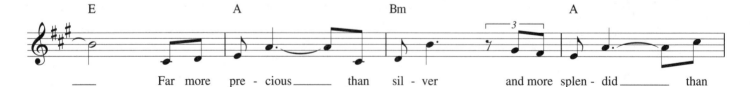

___ Far more pre - cious than sil - ver and more splen - did ___ than

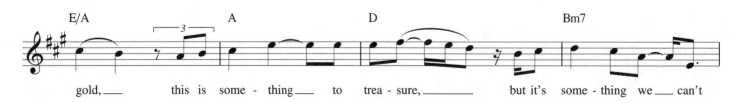

gold, ___ this is some - thing ___ to trea - sure, ___ but it's some - thing we ___ can't

© 1997 Wonderland Music Company, Inc.
All Rights Reserved   Used by Permission

shines _____ a - bove, _____ there'll al - ways be Christ - mas, _____

so there al - ways will be a time ___ when the world is filled with

peace and love. _____

Christmas Is a-Comin'
(May God Bless You)

Words and Music by Frank Luther

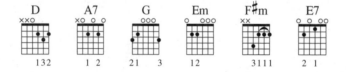

Strum Pattern: 3, 4
Pick Pattern: 4, 5

When I'm feel - in' blue, an'

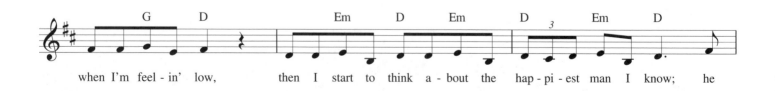

when I'm feel - in' low, then I start to think a - bout the hap - pi - est man I know; he

© 1953, 1956 (Renewed) FRANK MUSIC CORP.
All Rights Reserved

does-n't mind the snow an' he does-n't mind the rain, but all De-cem-ber you will hear him

at your win-dow pane, a-sing-in' a-gain an' a-gain an' a-gain an' a-gain an' a-gain an' a-gain.

Chorus

Christ-mas is a-com-in' and the geese are get-tin' fat, please to put a pen-ny in a
Christ-mas is a-com-in' and the lights are on the tree, how a-bout a tur-key leg for
Christ-mas is a-com-in' and the egg is in the nog, please to let me sit a-round your

poor man's hat, if you have-n't got a pen-ny then a ha' pen-ny, 'll do, if you
poor old me? If you have-n't got a tur-key leg a tur-key wing 'll do, if you
old yule log, if you'd rath-er I did-n't sit a-round, to stand a-round 'll do, if you'd

have-n't got a ha' pen-ny, may God bless you. God bless you, gen-tle-men,
have-n't got a tur-key wing, may God bless you. God bless you, gen-tle-men,
rath-er I did-n't stand a-round, may God bless you. God bless you, gen-tle-men,

God bless you, if you have-n't got a ha' pen-ny, may God bless you.
God bless you, if you have-n't got a tur-key wing, may God bless you.
God bless you, if you'd rath-er I did-n't stand a-round, may

Outro
Slowly

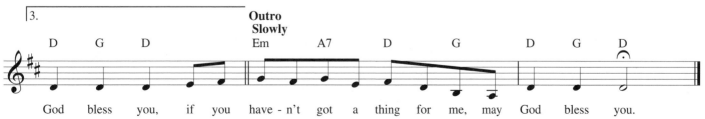

God bless you, if you have-n't got a thing for me, may God bless you.

Because It's Christmas
(For All the Children)

Music by Barry Manilow
Lyric by Bruce Sussman and Jack Feldman

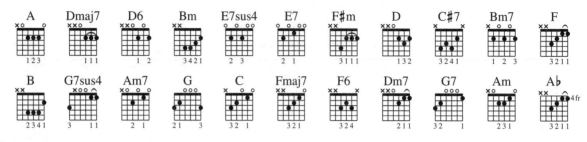

Strum Pattern: 4
Pick Pattern: 3

Verse
Moderately slow

1. To-night the stars shine for the chil - dren and light the way for dreams to
2. *See additional lyrics*

fly. To-night our love comes wrapped in rib - bons.

The world is right and hopes are high. And from a dark and frost - ed

win - dow a child ap - pears to search the sky be - cause it's

Christ-mas, be-cause it's Christ-mas. Christ-mas for now and for-ev - er for all of the

chil - dren and for the chil - dren in us all.

Copyright © 1986 by Careers-BMG Music Publishing, Inc., Appoggiatura Music and Camp Songs Music
All Rights Administered by Careers-BMG Music Publishing, Inc.
International Copyright Secured All Rights Reserved

Additional Lyrics

2. Tonight belongs to all the children.
   Tonight their joy rings through the air.
   And so, we send our tender blessings
   To all the children ev'rywhere
   To see the smiles and hear the laughter,
   A time to give, a time to share
   Because it's Christmas for now and forever
   For all of the children in us all.

Caroling, Caroling

Words by Wihla Hutson
Music by Alfred Burt

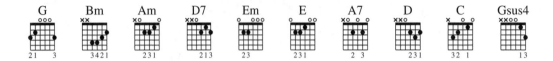

Strum Pattern: 8
Pick Pattern: 8

Verse
Moderately fast

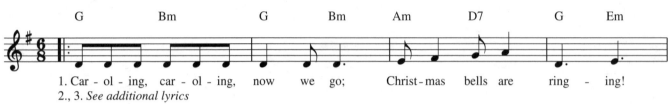

1. Car - ol - ing, car - ol - ing, now we go; Christ - mas bells are ring - ing!
2., 3. *See additional lyrics*

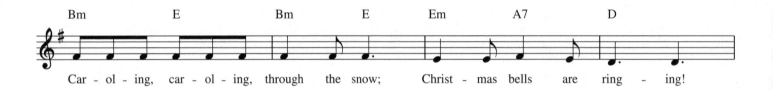

Car - ol - ing, car - ol - ing, through the snow; Christ - mas bells are ring - ing!

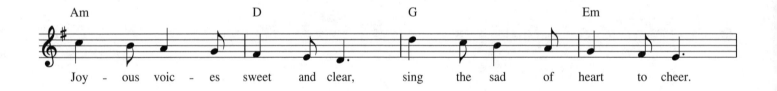

Joy - ous voic - es sweet and clear, sing the sad of heart to cheer.

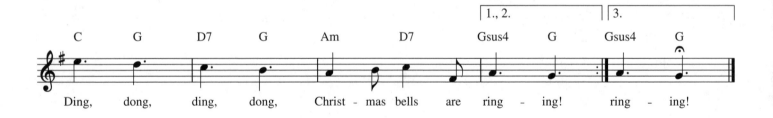

Ding, dong, ding, dong, Christ - mas bells are ring - ing! ring - ing!

Additional Lyrics

2. Caroling, caroling, through the town;
   Christmas bells are ringing!
   Caroling, caroling, up and down;
   Christmas bells are ringing!
   Mark ye well the song we sing,
   Gladsome tidings now we bring.
   Ding, dong, ding, dong,
   Christmas Bells are ringing!

3. Caroling, caroling, near and far;
   Christmas bells are ringing!
   Following, following yonder star;
   Christmas bells are ringing!
   Sing we all this happy morn,
   "Lo, the King of heav'n is born!"
   Ding, dong, ding, dong,
   Christmas bells are ringing!

TRO- © Copyright 1954 (Renewed) and 1957 (Renewed) Hollis Music, Inc., New York, NY
International Copyright Secured
All Rights Reserved Including Public Performance For Profit
Used by Permission

The Chipmunk Song

Words and Music by Ross Bagdasarian

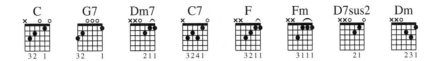

Strum Pattern: 8
Pick Pattern: 8

Happily

Christ - mas, Christ - mas time is near. Time for toys and

time for cheer. We've been good but we can't last.

Hur - ry Christ - mas, hur - ry fast! Want a plane that

loops the loop. Me, I want a hu - la hoop. We can

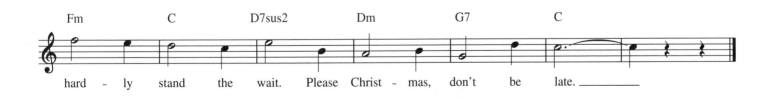

hard - ly stand the wait. Please Christ - mas, don't be late. _____

Copyright © 1958 by Bagdasarian Productions LLC
Copyright Renewed
All Rights Controlled and Administered by Bagdasarian Productions LLC
All Rights Reserved   Used by Permission

C-H-R-I-S-T-M-A-S

Words by Jenny Lou Carson
Music by Eddy Arnold

Strum Pattern: 3
Pick Pattern: 3

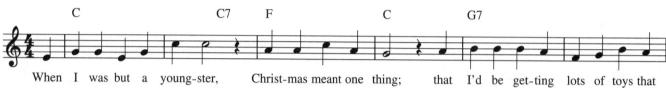

When I was but a young-ster, Christ-mas meant one thing; that I'd be get-ting lots of toys that

day. _____ I learned a whole lot dif-f'rent when Moth-er sat me down and taught me to spell

Chorus

Christ-mas this way. _____ "C" is for the Christ child born up-on this day,

"H" for her-ald an-gels in the night. _____ "R" means our Re-deem-er, "I" means Is-ra-

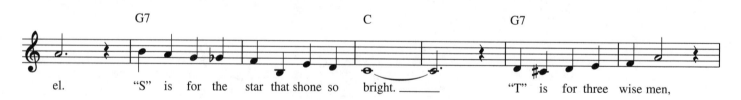

el. "S" is for the star that shone so bright. _____ "T" is for three wise men,

they who trav-eled far. "M" is for the man-ger where He lay. _____ "A"'s for all He

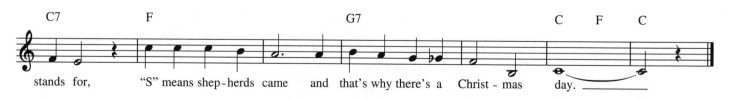

stands for, "S" means shep-herds came and that's why there's a Christ-mas day. _____

Copyright © 1949 by Hill & Range Songs, Inc.
Copyright Renewed
All Rights Administered by Unichappell Music Inc.
International Copyright Secured   All Rights Reserved

Christmas Is Just About Here

Words and Music by Loonis McGlohon

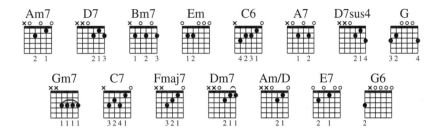

Strum Pattern: 4
Pick Pattern: 3

Verse
Joyfully

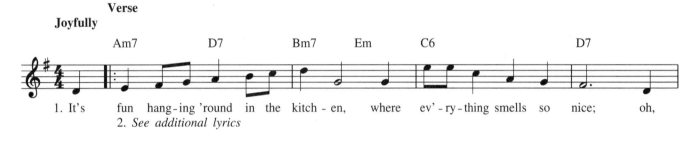

1. It's fun hang-ing 'round in the kitch-en, where ev'-ry-thing smells so nice; oh,
2. *See additional lyrics*

Ma-ma is bak-ing a fruit-cake with ap-ples, hon-ey and spice. The

chil-dren are get-ting ex-cit-ed when-ev-er gray clouds ap-pear; the

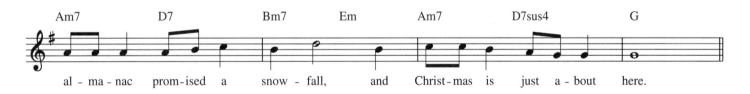

al-ma-nac prom-ised a snow-fall, and Christ-mas is just a-bout here.

Chorus

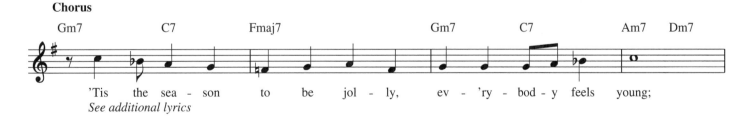

'Tis the sea-son to be jol-ly, ev-'ry-bod-y feels young;
See additional lyrics

deck the halls with boughs of hol-ly and let the stock-ings get hung. We'll

TRO - © Copyright 1984 and 1985 Melody Trails, Inc., New York, NY
International Copyright Secured
All Rights Reserved Including Public Performance For Profit
Used by Permission

15

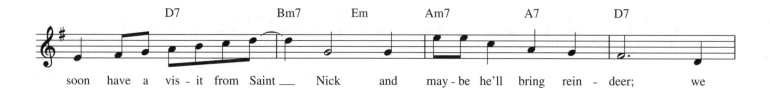

soon have a vis-it from Saint ___ Nick and may-be he'll bring rein - deer; we

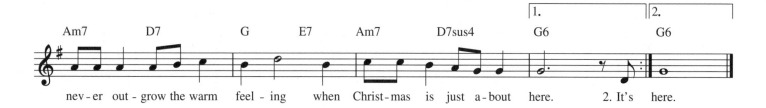

nev-er out-grow the warm feel-ing when Christ-mas is just a-bout here. 2. It's here.

Additional Lyrics

2. It's great fun when Papa will take us
To pick out a Christmas tree;
Mom says to be sure that we
Choose one that's big and taller than me.
It's time to start wrapping the presents
For ev'ryone we hold dear;
Then hiding them back in the closet
'Cause Christmas is just about here.

Chorus Deck the halls with boughs of holly,
Fill up the candy jar;
Light a candle in the window
And hang up the Christmas star.
I like ev'rything about Christmas,
The holly and the holiday cheer;
Let's hurry up and get ready
'Cause Christmas is just about here.

The Christmas Song
(Chestnuts Roasting on an Open Fire)
Music and Lyric by Mel Torme and Robert Wells

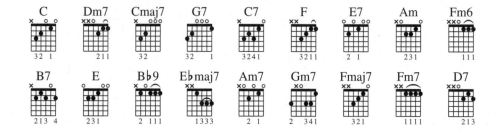

Strum Pattern: 2
Pick Pattern: 3

Verse
Sentimentally

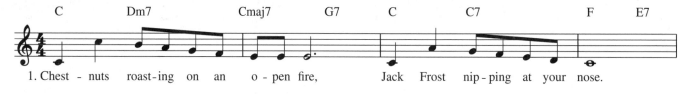

1. Chest - nuts roast-ing on an o-pen fire, Jack Frost nip-ping at your nose.

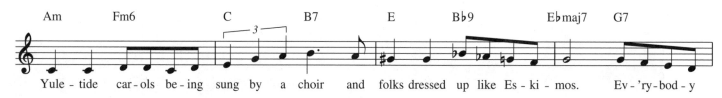

Yule - tide car-ols be-ing sung by a choir and folks dressed up like Es-ki-mos. Ev-'ry-bod-y

© 1946 (Renewed) EDWIN H. MORRIS & COMPANY, A Division of MPL Communications, Inc.
All Rights Reserved

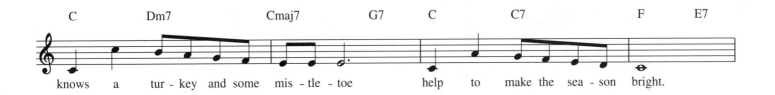

knows a tur-key and some mis-tle-toe help to make the sea-son bright.

Ti - ny tots with their eyes all a - glow will find it hard to sleep to - night. They know that

Bridge

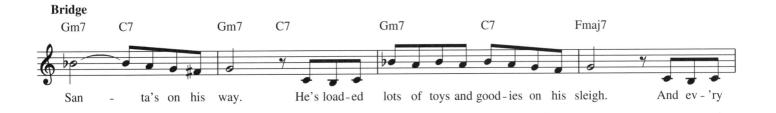

San - ta's on his way. He's load-ed lots of toys and good-ies on his sleigh. And ev-'ry

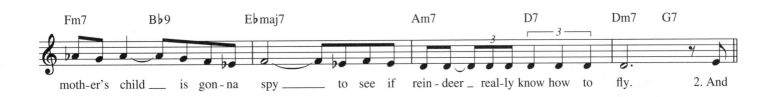

moth-er's child __ is gon-na spy _____ to see if rein-deer _ real-ly know how to fly. 2. And

Verse

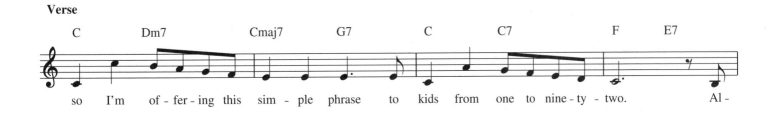

so I'm of-fer-ing this sim-ple phrase to kids from one to nine-ty - two. Al -

though it's been said man - y times, man - y ways, "Mer - ry Christ - mas to you."

The Christmas Shoes

Words and Music by Leonard Ahlstrom and Eddie Carswell

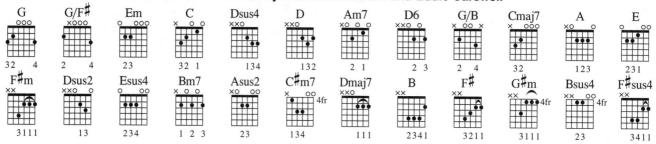

Strum Pattern: 3
Pick Pattern: 3

Verse
Moderately

1. It was al - most Christ - mas time; __ there I stood in an - oth - er line, __

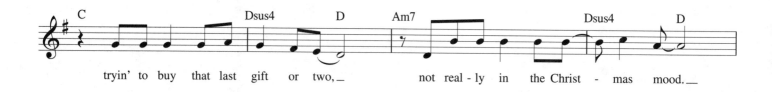

tryin' to buy that last gift or two, __ not real - ly in the Christ - mas mood. __

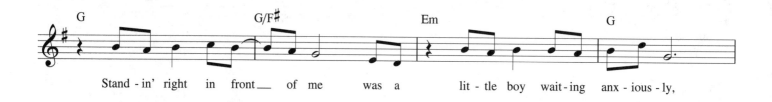

Stand - in' right in front __ of me was a lit - tle boy wait - ing anx - ious - ly,

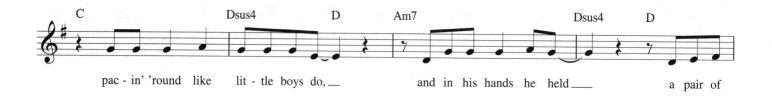

pac - in' 'round like lit - tle boys do, __ and in his hands he held __ a pair of

shoes. And his clothes were worn and old, __ he was

Copyright © 2000 Sony/ATV Songs LLC, Jerry's Haven Music and WB Music Corp.
All Rights on behalf of Sony/ATV Songs LLC Administered by Sony/ATV Music Publishing, 8 Music Square West, Nashville, TN 37203
All Rights on behalf of Jerry's Haven Music Administered by WB Music Corp.
International Copyright Secured   All Rights Reserved

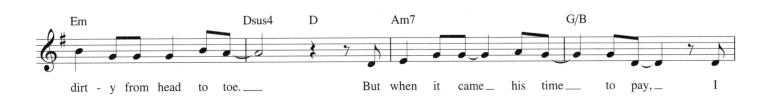

dirt - y from head to toe.___ But when it came___ his time___ to pay,___ I

Chorus

could - n't be - lieve___ what I heard him say. "Sir, I wan - na buy these shoes___

___ for my ma - ma, please.___ It's Christ - mas Eve___ and these

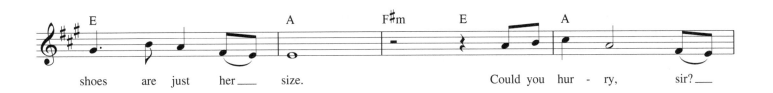

shoes are just her___ size. Could you hur - ry, sir?___

Dad - dy says there's not much time.___ You see, she's been sick for quite___

___ a while___ and I know these shoes will make___ her smile___ and I

want her to look beau - ti - ful___ if Ma - ma___ meets Je - sus___ to -

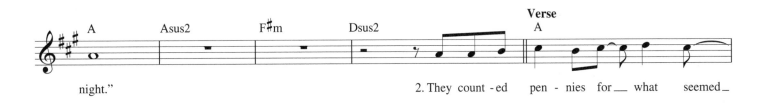

Verse

night." 2. They count - ed pen - nies for___ what seemed___

E   F#m   A

___ like years, ___ then the cash - ier said, "Son, there's not e - nough here." ___

Dsus2   Esus4   E   Bm7

He searched his pock - ets fran - ti - c'lly, ___ then he turned and he

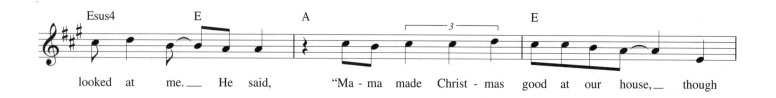

Esus4   E   A   *3*   E

looked at me. ___ He said, "Ma - ma made Christ - mas good at our house, ___ though

F#m   *3*   A   D   *3*   Esus4   E

most years she just did with - out. ___ Tell me, sir, what am I gon - na do? ___ Some

Bm7   Esus4   E   *3*   A

how I've got - ta buy ___ her these Christ - mas shoes."   So, I

F#m   Esus4   E   F#m   Esus4

laid the mon - ey down. ___ I just had to help ___ him out. ___ And I'll

Bm7   C#m7   Dmaj7   Esus4

nev - er for - get ___ the look on his face when he said, "Ma - ma's gon - na look so ___ great." ___

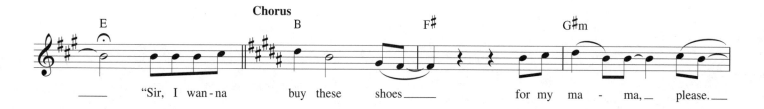

Chorus

E   B   F#   G#m

___ "Sir, I wan - na buy these shoes ___ for my ma - ma, ___ please. ___

It's Christ-mas Eve and these shoes are just her_ size.

Could you hur - ry, sir?_ Dad - dy says there's not much time._

_ You see, she's been sick for quite_ a while_ and I

know these shoes will make_ her smile_ and I want her to look beau -

- ti - ful_ if Ma - ma_ meets Je - sus_ to - night."_

Bridge

_ I knew I caught a glimpse_ of heav - en's love_ as he

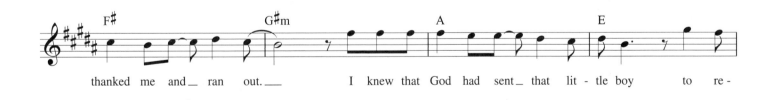

thanked me and_ ran out._ I knew that God had sent_ that lit - tle boy to re -

mind me_ what Christ - mas is all a - bout. _Children:_ "Sir, I wan - na

Chorus

buy these shoes _____ for my ma - ma, please. _____ It's

Christ - mas Eve _____ and these shoes are just _____ her _____ size. *Add lead vocal:* Could you

hur - ry, sir? _____ Dad - dy says there's not much time. _____ You see,

she's been sick for quite _____ a while _____ and I know these shoes will make _____

_____ her smile _____ and I want her to look beau - ti - ful _____ if

Ma - ma _____ meets Je - sus _____ to - night. *Boy:* I

want her to _____ look beau - ti - ful if Ma - ma _____ meets Je - sus

_____ to - night."

Christmas Time Is Here

from A CHARLIE BROWN CHRISTMAS
Words by Lee Mendelson
Music by Vince Guaraldi

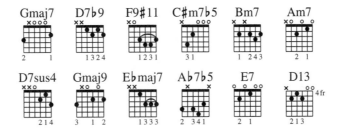

Strum Pattern: 7, 8
Pick Pattern: 7, 8

Additional lyrics

2. Snowflakes in the air,
   Carols ev'rywhere.
   Olden times and ancient rhymes
   Of love and dreams to share.

Copyright © 1966 LEE MENDELSON FILM PRODUCTIONS, INC.
Copyright Renewed
International Copyright Secured   All Rights Reserved

The Christmas Waltz

Words by Sammy Cahn
Music by Jule Styne

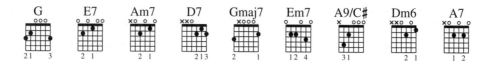

Strum Pattern: 9
Pick Pattern: 7

Verse

Moderately

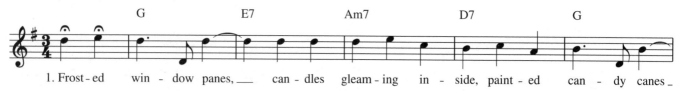

1. Frost-ed win-dow panes, ___ can-dles gleam-ing in - side, paint-ed can-dy canes ___

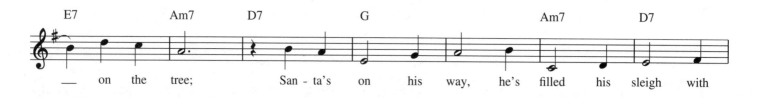

___ on the tree; San - ta's on his way, he's filled his sleigh with

Verse

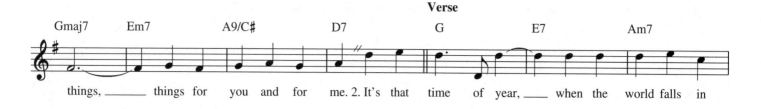

things, ___ things for you and for me. 2. It's that time of year, ___ when the world falls in

love. Ev - 'ry song you hear ___ seems to say: ___ "Mer - ry Christ - mas, ___ may your

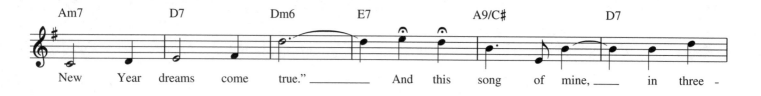

New Year dreams come true." ___ And this song of mine, ___ in three -

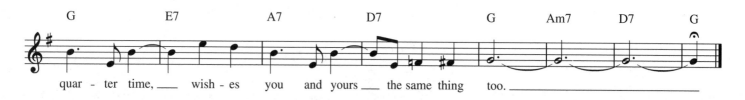

quar - ter time, ___ wish - es you and yours ___ the same thing too. ___

Copyright © 1954 by Producers Music Publishing Co. and Cahn Music Company
Copyright Renewed
All Rights for Producers Music Publishing Co. Administered by Chappell & Co.
All Rights for Cahn Music Company Administered by Cherry Lane Music Publishing Company, Inc. and DreamWorks Songs
International Copyright Secured   All Rights Reserved

Cold December Nights

Words and Music by Michael McCary and Shawn Stockman

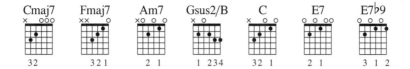

Strum Pattern: 6
Pick Pattern: 4

Moderately slow

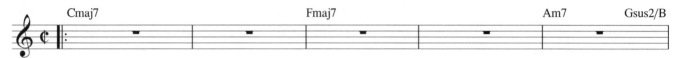

So cold, ___

___ so cold. ___ Oh. ___

1. Cold De - cem - ber nights___
2. The stars___ shine bright

___ like this makes___ me___ real - ly ___ scared. You're not real - ly ___ there
as the night air, ___ and the thought of you not be - ing here makes me shed a ___ tear.

and my tree is real - ly bare.___ An - oth - er lone - ly night,___ no gifts,
And yet mat - ters re - main un - clear 'bout why___ you're gone,___ or if you'll ev - er

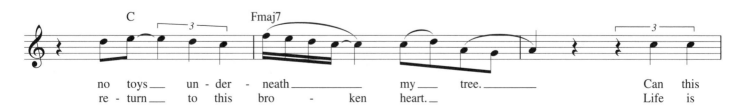

no toys ___ un - der - neath ___ my ___ tree. Can this
re - turn ___ to this bro - ken heart. ___ Life is

Copyright © 1993 by Black Panther Publishing Co., Slim Shot Publishing and Ensign Music Corporation
International Copyright Secured   All Rights Reserved

Am7 Gsus2/B C Fmaj7 E7 N.C.

real - ly ___ be? _____ I'm sing - ing Christ - mas car - ols and there's no Christ - mas for
so torn __ a - part _____ and God knows, __ God __ knows where I need to ___ start re -

Chorus
Am7 Gsus2/B C Fmaj7

me _____ } (Why aren't __ you next __ to me?) _____ ...cel - e - brat - ing
build - ing. _____

Am7 Gsus2/B C Fmaj7

Christ - mas? ____ (Why can't __ you see ___ what hurts so bad?) ____ Whoa. ____

Am7 Gsus2/B C Fmaj7
3

____ How __ can you go ___ with - out __ pay - ing mind __ to my sor - row ____

Am Gsus2/B C Fmaj7 E7♭9

____ on this cold __ De - cem - ber night? ____
(You can't im - ag - ine how, how I feel.) _____

1.
N.C.

_____ Ooh. _____

2. **Interlude**
N.C. Cmaj7

Oh. _____

Fmaj7 Am7 Gsus2/B C Fmaj7

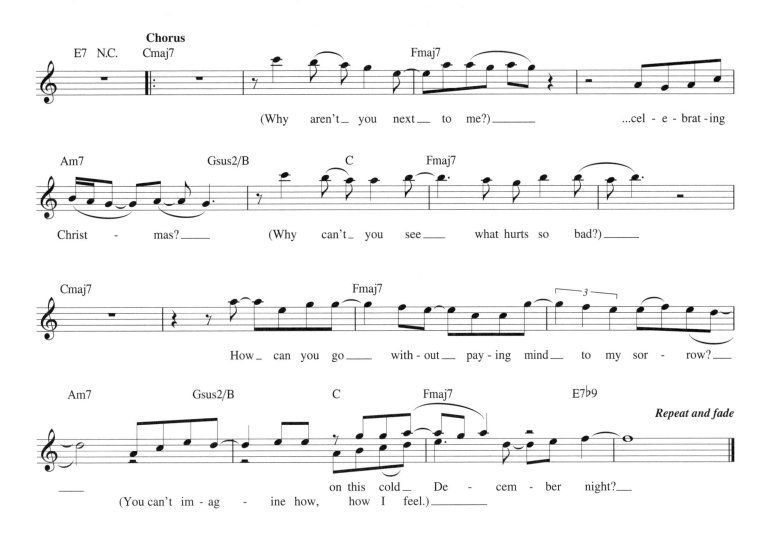

(Why aren't you next to me?) ...cel-e-brat-ing

Christ-mas? (Why can't you see what hurts so bad?)

How can you go with-out pay-ing mind to my sor-row?

Repeat and fade

(You can't im-ag-ine how, how I feel.) on this cold De-cem-ber night?

Do They Know It's Christmas?

Words and Music by M. Ure and B. Geldof

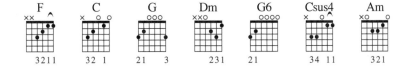

Strum Pattern: 3, 4
Pick Pattern: 3, 4

Verse

Moderate Rock

It's Christ-mas time, there's no need to be a-fraid.

At Christ-mas time, we let in light and we ban-ish shade.

Copyright © 1984 by M. Ure and B. Geldof
All Rights Administered by Chappell & Co.
International Copyright Secured   All Rights Reserved

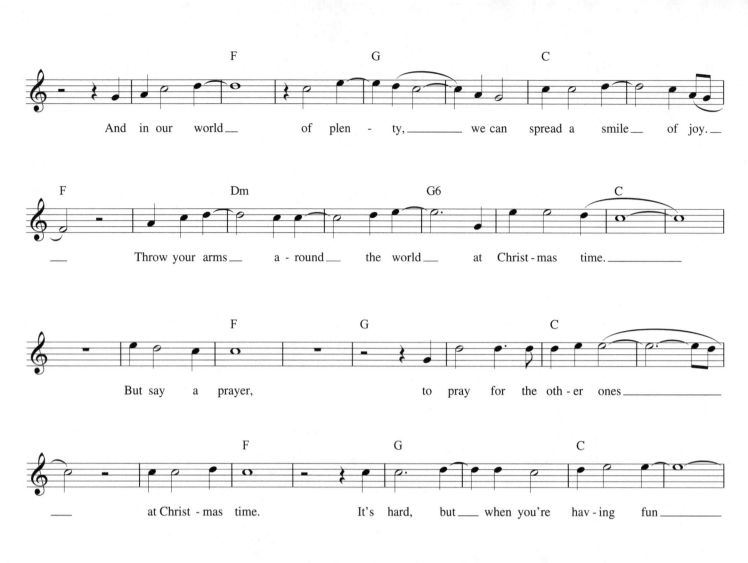

And in our world ___ of plen - ty, _____ we can spread a smile ___ of joy. ___

___ Throw your arms ___ a - round ___ the world ___ at Christ - mas time. _____

But say a prayer, to pray for the oth - er ones _____

___ at Christ - mas time. It's hard, but ___ when you're hav - ing fun _____

___ there's ___ a ___ world out - side your win - dow, and it's a world of ___ dread and fear ___

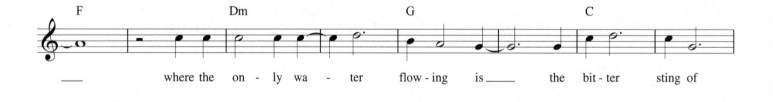

___ where the on - ly wa - ter flow - ing is ___ the bit - ter sting of

tears. And the Christ - mas bells ___ that ring ___ there ___ are the clang - ing chimes of doom. ___

___ Well, to - night thank God it's them ___ in - stead of you. _____

Do You Hear What I Hear

Words and Music by Noel Regney and Gloria Shayne

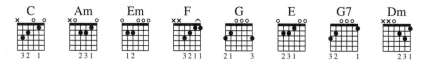

Strum Pattern: 4
Pick Pattern: 3

Additional Lyrics

2. Said the little lamb to the shepherd boy,
   Do you hear what I hear?
   Ringing through the sky, shepherd boy,
   Do you hear what I hear?
   A song, a song, high above the tree,
   With a voice as big as the sea,
   With a voice as big as the sea.

3. Said the shepherd boy to the mighty king,
   Do you know what I know?
   In your palace warm, mighty king,
   Do you know what I know?
   A Child, a Child shivers in the cold,
   Let us bring Him silver and gold,
   Let us bring Him silver and gold.

4. Said the king to the people ev'rywhere,
   Listen to what I say!
   Pray for peace, people ev'rywhere,
   Listen to what I say?
   The Child, the Child, sleeping in the night;
   He will bring us goodness and light,
   He will bring us goodness and light.

Copyright © 1962 by Regent Music Corporation (BMI)
Copyright Renewed by Jewel Music Publishing Co., Inc. (ASCAP)
International Copyright Secured   All Rights Reserved
Used by Permission

Emmanuel

Words and Music by Michael W. Smith

*Strum Pattern: 2
*Pick Pattern: 4

© 1983 MEADOWGREEN MUSIC COMPANY
Admin. by EMI CHRISTIAN MUSIC PUBLISHING
All Rights Reserved   Used by Permission

Frosty the Snow Man

Words and Music by Steve Nelson and Jack Rollins

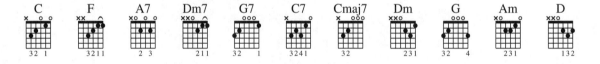

Strum Pattern: 3, 2
Pick Pattern: 3, 4

Verse
Moderately fast

1. Frost - y, the snow man was a jol - ly hap - py soul, with a
3. Frost - y, the snow man knew the sun was hot that day, so he

corn cob pipe and a but - ton nose and two eyes made out of coal.
said, "Let's run and we'll have some fun now be - fore I melt a - way."

Copyright © 1950 by Chappell & Co.
Copyright Renewed
International Copyright Secured   All Rights Reserved

C   F   C

Frost - y   the snow man   is a fair - y tale they say.   He was
Down   to the vil - lage   with a broom - stick in his hand,   run - ning

F   C   A7   Dm7   G7   C   G7

made of snow but the chil - dren know how he came to life one day.   There
here and there all a - round the square, say - in' "Catch me if you can."   He

Bridge

F   Cmaj7   Dm   G7   C

must have been some mag - ic in that old silk hat they found,   for
let them down the streets of town right to the traf - fic cop,   and he

G   Am   D   G   G7

when they placed it on his head he be - gan to dance a - round.   2. Oh,
on - ly paused a mo - ment when ___ he heard him hol - ler, "Stop"!   4. For

Verse

C   F   C

Frost - y   the snow man   was a - live as he could be,   and the
Frost - y   the snow man   had to hur - ry on his way,   but he

F   C   A7   Dm7   G7   C   G7

chil - dren say he could laugh and play just the same as you and me.
waved good - bye say - in', "Don't you cry, I'll be back a - gain some day."

Outro

C   G7

Thump-et - y thump thump, thump-et - y thump thump, look at Frost - y go.

C

Thump-et - y thump thump, thump-et - y thump thump, o - ver the hills of snow.

Feliz Navidad

Music and Lyrics by José Feliciano

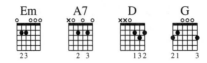

Strum Pattern: 2, 1
Pick Pattern: 4, 2

Copyright © 1970 J & H Publishing Company (ASCAP)
Copyright Renewed
All Rights Administered by Stollman and Stollman o/b/o J & H Publishing Company
International Copyright Secured   All Rights Reserved

The Gift

Words and Music by Stephanie Davis

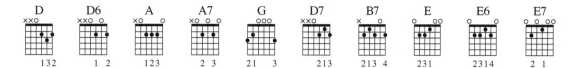

Strum Pattern: 8
Pick Pattern: 8

Intro
Moderately

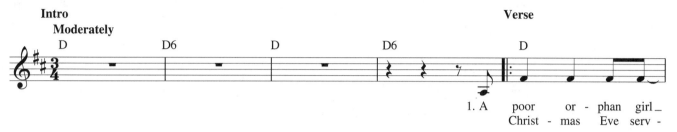

1. A poor or-phan girl_
Christ-mas Eve serv-

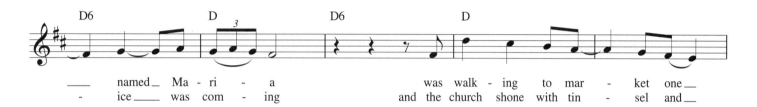

___ named_ Ma-ri-a was walk-ing to mar-ket one_
-ice___ was com-ing and the church shone with tin-sel and__

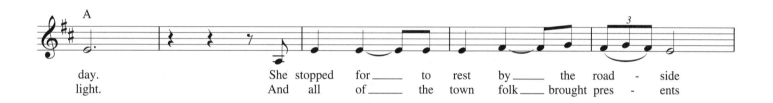

day. She stopped for ___ to rest by ___ the road-side
light. And all of ___ the town folk ___ brought pres-ents

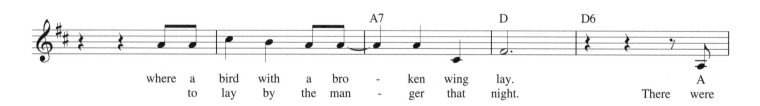

where a bird with a bro-ken wing lay. A
to lay by the man-ger that night. There were

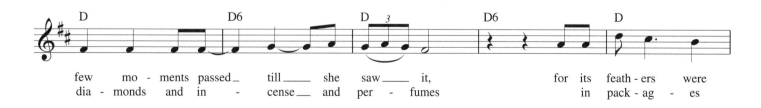

few mo-ments passed_ till ___ she saw ___ it, for its feath-ers were
dia-monds and in-cense ___ and per-fumes in pack-ag-es

cov-ered_ with sand.___ But soon, clean_ and wrapped, it ___ was
fit for ___ a king.___ But for one rag-ged bird in ___ a

© 1990 EMI BLACKWOOD MUSIC INC. and BEARTOOTH MUSIC
All Rights Controlled and Administered by EMI BLACKWOOD MUSIC INC.
All Rights Reserved   International Copyright Secured   Used by Permission

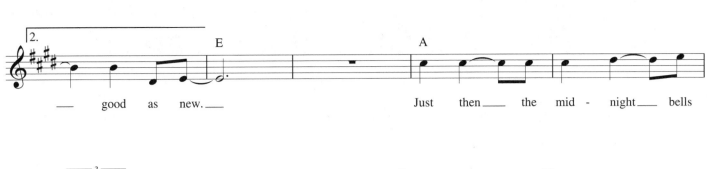

good as new. Just then the mid - night bells

rang out and the lit - tle bird start - ed to

sing a song that no words could re -

cap - ture, whose beau - ty was fit for a king.

Now Ma - ri - a felt blessed just to

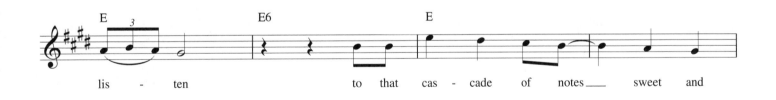

lis - ten to that cas - cade of notes sweet and

long, as her of - f'ring was lift - ed to

heav - en by the ver - y first night - in - gale's song.

The First Chanukah Night

Words by Enid Futterman Music by Michael Cohen

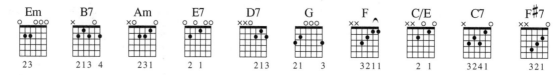

Strum Pattern: 4
Pick Pattern: 1

1. On the first Cha - nu - kah night we light one Cha - nu - kah light in

mem - 'ry of the mir - a - cle of the first Cha - nu - kah night. On the

sec - ond Cha - nu - kah night we light two Cha - nu - kah lights in

mem - 'ry of the mir - a - cle of the sec - ond Cha - nu - kah night. 2. On the

third Cha - nu - kah night we light three Cha - nu - kah lights in

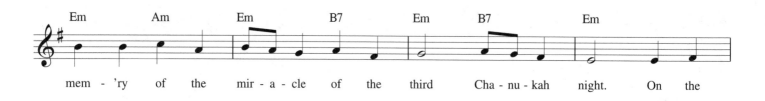

mem - 'ry of the mir - a - cle of the third Cha - nu - kah night. On the

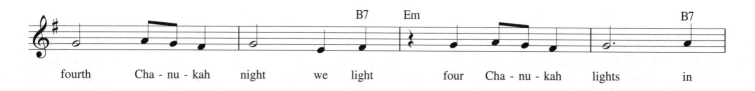

fourth Cha - nu - kah night we light four Cha - nu - kah lights in

Copyright © 1985 by Enid Futterman and Michael Cohen
Williamson Music administrator of all rights on behalf of itself and Jem Associates throughout the world
International Copyright Secured   All Rights Reserved

The Gift

Words and Music by Tom Douglas and Jim Brickman

Strum Pattern: 3, 6
Pick Pattern: 4

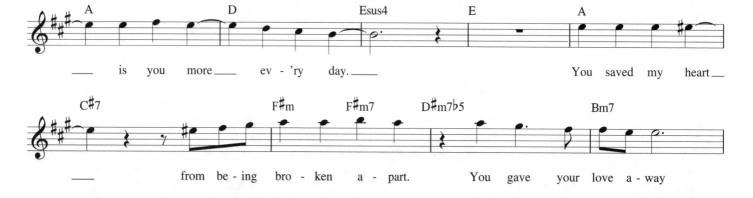

Copyright © 1997 Sony/ATV Songs LLC, Multisongs, Inc. and Brickman Arrangement
All Rights on behalf of Sony/ATV Songs LLC Administered by Sony/ATV Music Publishing, 8 Music Square West, Nashville, TN 37203
All Rights on behalf of Brickman Arrangement Administered by Multisongs, Inc.
International Copyright Secured All Rights Reserved

love a - way   and I'm thank - ful ev - 'ry day   for the

Interlude

gift.

D.S. al Coda

All I want

Coda

_____ You gave your love a - way.   I can't find the words to say

that I'm thank - ful ___ ev - 'ry day ___   for the gift.

Ooh, _____ ah. _____ Ah, _____ ooh, _____ ooh. _____

Grandma's Killer Fruitcake

Words and Music by Elmo Shropshire and Rita Abrams

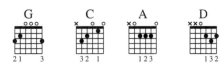

Strum Pattern: 3
Pick Pattern: 5

Intro

Country Polka

1. The

Verse

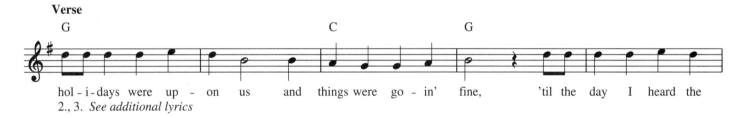

hol - i - days were up - on us and things were go - in' fine, 'til the day I heard the
2., 3. See additional lyrics

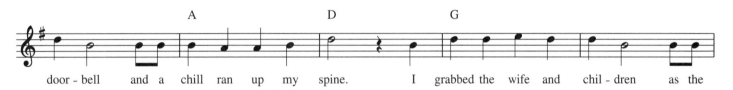

door - bell and a chill ran up my spine. I grabbed the wife and chil - dren as the

post - man wheeled it in. A year - ly Christ - mas night - mare has just come back a -

Chorus

gain. It was hard - er than the head of Un - cle Buck - y, heav - y as a ser - mon of

Preach - er Luck - y, One's e - nough to give the whole state of Ken - tuck - y a

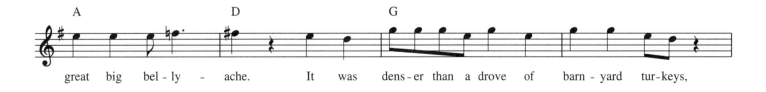

great big bel - ly - ache. It was dens - er than a drove of barn - yard tur - keys,

Copyright © 1992 Elmo Publishing and Mill Valley Music
International Copyright Secured   All Rights Reserved

tough-er than a truck load of all beef jerk - y. Dri - er than a drought in Al - bu - quer - que,

1., 2. **3.**

Grand - ma's kil - ler fruit - cake. cake.

Additional Lyrics

2. Now I've had to swallow some marginal fare at our family feast.
   I even downed Aunt Dolly's possom pie just to keep the family peace.
   I winced at Wilma's gizzard mousse, but said it tasted fine.
   But that lethal weapon that Grandma bakes is where I drew the line.

3. It's early Christmas morning, the phone rings us awake.
   It's Grandma, Pa, she wants to know how'd we like the cake.
   "Well, Grandma, I never. Uh we couldn't. It was, uh, unbelievable, that's for shore.
   What's that you say? Oh, no Grandma, Puh-leez don't send us more!"

Greenwillow Christmas

from GREENWILLOW
By Frank Loesser

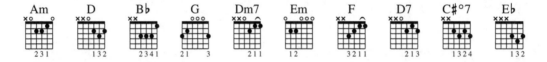

Strum Pattern: 4
Pick Pattern: 3

Verse

Moderately

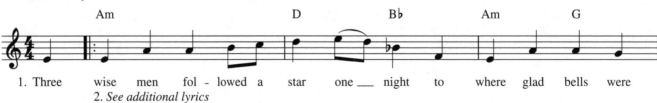

1. Three wise men fol - lowed a star one ___ night to where glad bells were
2. *See additional lyrics*

peal - ing, ___ and soon be - held the ___ Ho - ly ___ Child and

© 1959, 1960 (Renewed) FRANK MUSIC CORP.
All Rights Reserved

all the shep-herds kneel - ing. ____ Come see ____ the

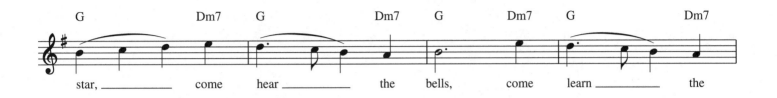

star, ____ come hear ____ the bells, come learn ____ the

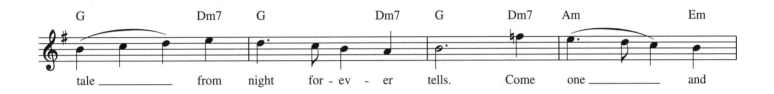

tale ____ from night for-ev-er tells. Come one ____ and

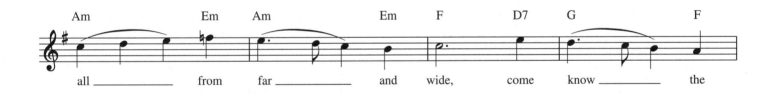

all ____ from far ____ and wide, come know ____ the

joy, ____ the joy, ____ the joy, ____ come know ____ the

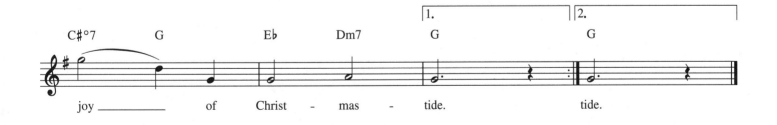

joy ____ of Christ - mas - tide. tide.

Additional Lyrics

2. 'Twas long ago in Bethlehem
Yet ever live the glory,
And hearts all glow and voices rise
A-caroling the story.

Give Love on Christmas Day

Words and Music by Freddie Perren, Alphonso Mizell, Christine Yarian, Barry Gordy and Deke Richards

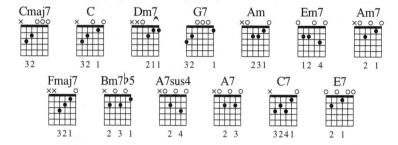

*Strum Pattern: 1, 2
*Pick Pattern: 4

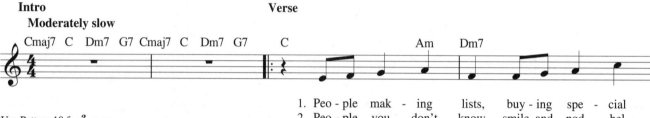

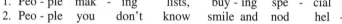

*Use Pattern 10 for $\frac{2}{4}$ meas.

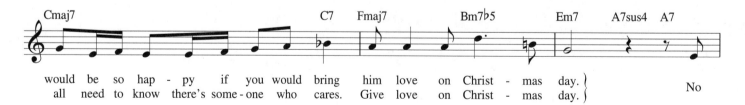

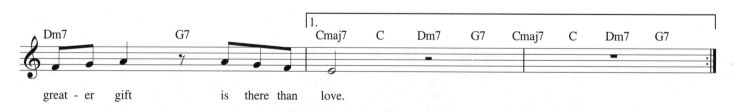

© 1970 (Renewed 1998) JOBETE MUSIC CO., INC.
All Rights Controlled and Administered by EMI APRIL MUSIC INC.
All Rights Reserved   International Copyright Secured   Used by Permission

love. What the world needs is love, yes, the world needs your

love. Why don't you give love on Christ - mas day? Oh,

ev - 'ry lit - tle child on San - ta's knee has room for your love un - der - neath his tree. Give love on Christ - mas

day. No great - er gift is there than love. What the love.

Glad Tidings
(Shalom Chaverim)

English Lyrics and New Music Arranged by Ronnie Gilbert, Lee Hays, Fred Hellerman and Pete Seeger

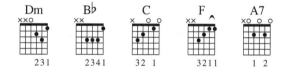

Strum Pattern: 4
Pick Pattern: 3

Verse

Moderately

1. Sha - lom cha - ve - rim, sha - lom cha - ve - rim, sha - lom, sha - lom, I'

ti - dings we bring of peace on ___ earth, good will toward men of

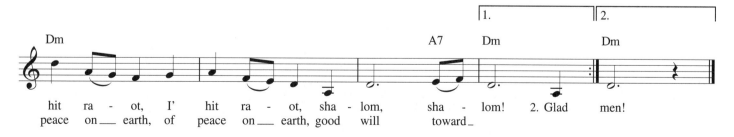

hit ra - ot, I' hit ra - ot, sha - lom, sha - lom! 2. Glad men!

peace on ___ earth, of peace on ___ earth, good will toward ___

TRO - © Copyright 1951 (Renewed) Folkways Music Publishers, Inc., New York, NY
International Copyright Secured
All Rights Reserved Including Public Performance For Profit
Used by Permission

Goin' on a Sleighride

Words and Music by Ralph Blane

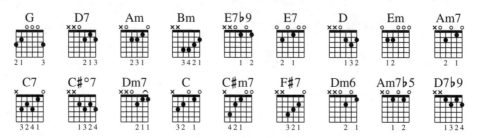

Strum Pattern: 10
Pick Pattern: 10

Verse
Moderately fast

We've got the sleigh-bells, _ the win-ter sea-son sleigh-bells. Hear those sleigh-bells ring-ing

merri-ly ev-'ry-where we go. _____ We've got the hors-es, _____ the

smart-est team of hors-es 'cause they know their way back home through all the ice and snow. _

_ We've got a com-fort, _ a fan-cy quilt-ed com-fort. If we

hit a lit-tle storm it's gon-na keep us warm. _ Ev'-ry-bod-y's

go-in', _____ hearts are o-ver-flow-in'. _____ Start you har-mo-niz-in', that's a

Strum Pattern: 3
Pick Pattern: 4

Chorus

full moon ris-in'. Why don't you come a-long? _ We're go-in' on a

Copyright © 1952 by Ralph Blane
Copyright Renewed, Assigned to Chappell & Co.
International Copyright Secured   All Rights Reserved

Grandma Got Run Over by a Reindeer

Words and Music by Randy Brooks

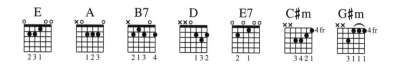

Strum Pattern: 3
Pick Pattern: 3

Chorus
Moderately bright

Grand-ma got run o-ver by a rein-deer walk-ing home from our house Christ-mas

Eve. You can say there's no such thing as San-ta, but

To Coda ⊕   **Verse**

as for me and Grand-pa, we be-lieve.

1. She'd been drink-ing too much
2., 3. *See additional lyrics*

egg-nog and we begged her not to go.

But she for-got her med-i-ca-tion, and she stag-gered out the door in-to the

snow. When we found her Christ-mas morn-ing

Copyright © 1984 by Kris Publishing (SESAC) and Elmo Publishing (SESAC)
Admin. by ICG
All Rights Reserved   Used by Permission

at the scene of the at - tack, she had hoof - prints on her

1., 2. **3.**

D.C. al Coda

fore - head, and in - crim - i - nat - ing Claus marks on her back. elves.

⊕ **Coda**

Outro-Chorus

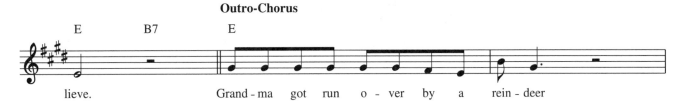

lieve. Grand - ma got run o - ver by a rein - deer

walk - ing home from our house Christ - mas Eve. You can say there's no such thing as

San - ta, but as for me and Grand - pa, we be - lieve. _____

Additional Lyrics

2. Now we're all so proud of Grandpa.
   He's been taking it so well.
   See him in there watching football,
   Drinking beer and playing cards with Cousin Mel.
   It's not Christmas without Grandma.
   All the family's dressed in black,
   And we just can't help but wonder:
   Should we open up her gifts or send them back?

3. Now the goose is on the table,
   And the pudding made of fig.
   And the blue and silver candles,
   That would just have matched the hair in Grandma's wig.
   I've warned all my friends and neighbors.
   Better watch out for yourselves.
   They should never give a license
   To a man who drives a sleigh and plays with elves.

The Greatest Gift of All

Words and Music by John Jarvis

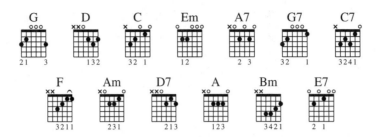

Strum Pattern: 4, 3
Pick Pattern: 5, 3

Verse

Moderately slow

1. Dawn is slow - ly break - ing, our friends have all __ gone home.

You and I are wait - ing for San - ta Claus to come.

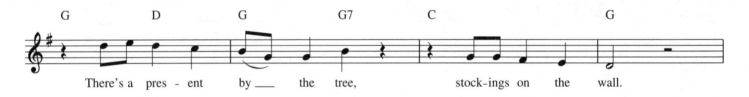

There's a pres - ent by __ the tree, stock-ings on the wall.

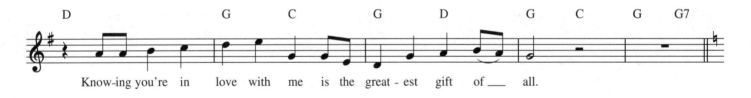

Know-ing you're in love with me is the great - est gift of __ all.

Verse

2. The fire is slow - ly fad - ing, __ chill is in the air.

All the gifts are wait - ing __ for chil - dren ev - 'ry - where.

Copyright © 1984 Sony/ATV Songs LLC
All Rights Administered by Sony/ATV Music Publishing, 8 Music Square West, Nashville, TN 37203
International Copyright Secured   All Rights Reserved

Through the win - dow I ___ can see ___ snow be - gin to fall.

Know-ing you're in ___ love with me ___ is the great - est gift of ___ all.

Verse

3. Just be - fore I go to sleep _____ I hear a church bell ring.

Mer - ry Christ - mas ev - 'ry - one _____ is the song it ___ sings.

So I say a si - lent prayer _____ for crea - tures great and small.

Peace on earth good _ will to men is the great - est gift of ___ all. Peace on earth good _

will to men is the great - est gift of ___ all. _____

*Use Pattern 10

Grown-Up Christmas List

Words and Music by David Foster and Linda Thompson-Jenner

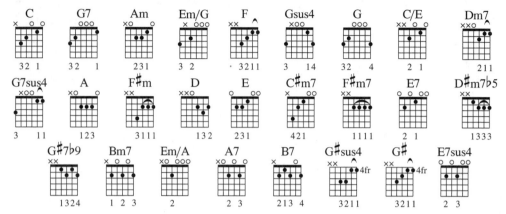

*Strum Pattern: 2
*Pick Pattern: 4

Intro
Slowly, freely

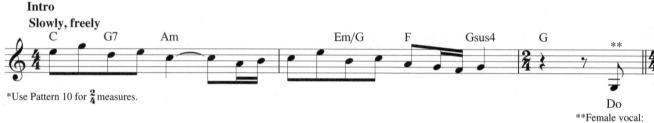

*Use Pattern 10 for 2/4 measures.

Do

****Female vocal:
sung one octave
higher than written**

Verse

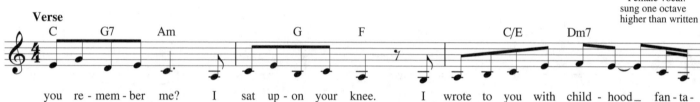

you re-mem-ber me? I sat up-on your knee. I wrote to you with child-hood__ fan-ta-

sies. Well, I'm all___ grown up now. Can you still help some-how? I'm

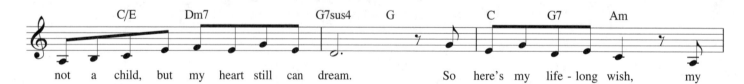

not a child, but my heart still can dream. So here's my life-long wish, my

grown-up___ Christ-mas list. Not for my-self, but for a world in need.

Chorus
Moderately slow, in time

No more lives___ torn a-part, that wars would nev-er start, and time would heal all

Copyright © 1990 by Air Bear Music, Warner-Tamerlane Publishing Corp. and Linda's Boys Music
All Rights for Air Bear Music Administered by Peermusic Ltd.
All Rights for Linda's Boys Music Administered by Warner-Tamerlane Publishing Corp.
International Copyright Secured   All Rights Reserved

hearts.   Ev - 'ry man would have a friend, that right would al - ways win,   and love would nev - er

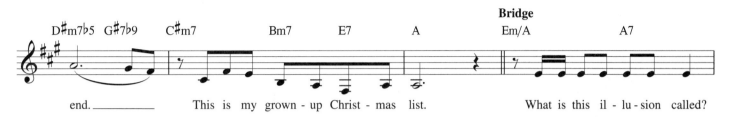

Bridge

end._____   This is my grown - up Christ - mas list.   What is this il - lu - sion called?

The in - no - cence of youth.   May - be on - ly in that blind be - lief can we ev - er find the   truth.____

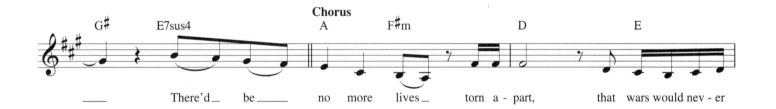

Chorus

____ There'd_ be ____ no more lives_ torn a - part,   that wars would nev - er

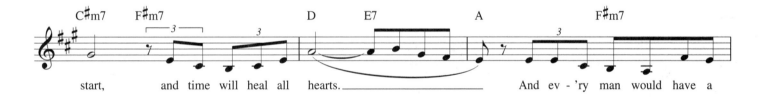

start,   and time will heal all hearts._____   And ev - 'ry man would have a

friend,   and right would al - ways_ win,   and love would nev - er____ end._____

__ This is my grown - up Christ - mas list. This is my on - ly life - long wish.__   This is ___ my grown - up

Slowly

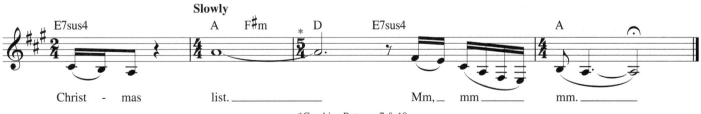

Christ - mas   list._____   Mm,_ mm ____ mm.

*Combine Patterns 7 & 10

Happy Christmas, Little Friend

Lyrics by Oscar Hammerstein II
Music by Richard Rodgers

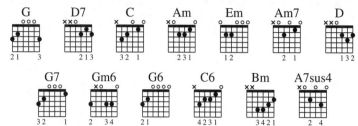

*Strum Pattern: 4
*Pick Pattern: 3

Verse
Moderately

The soft morn-ing light of a pale win-ter sun is trac-ing the trees on the snow, leap

*Use Pattern 8 for 3/4 measures.

up lit-tle friend and fly down the stairs for Christ-mas is wait-ing be-low. There's a

tree in the room run-ning o-ver with stars that twin-kle and sing to your eyes and

un-der the tree there are pres-ents that say un-wrap me and get a sur-

Chorus

prise. _____ Hap-py Christ-mas

lit-tle friend, may your heart be laugh-ing _____ all day. _____

Copyright © 1952 by The Rodgers & Hammerstein Foundation
Copyright Renewed
WILLIAMSON MUSIC owner of publication and allied rights throughout the world
International Copyright Secured   All Rights Reserved

May your joy be a dream you'll re-mem - ber, _____ as the

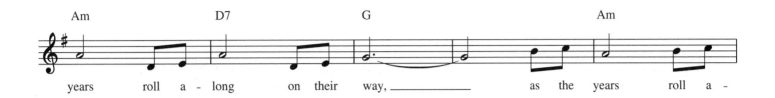

years roll a - long on their way, _____ as the years roll a -

long on their way, _____ you'll be show - ing your own kid ___ a

tree. _____ Then at last, my friend, you'll

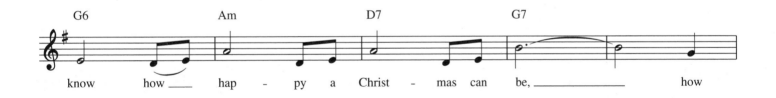

know how ___ hap - py a Christ - mas can be, _____ how

hap - py a Christ - mas can be. _____

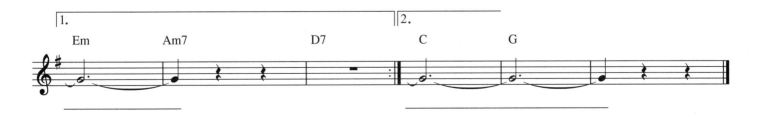

Happy Holiday

from the Motion Picture Irving Berlin's HOLIDAY INN
Words and Music by Irving Berlin

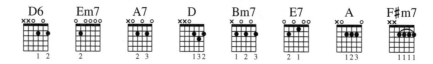

Strum Pattern: 3, 2
Pick Pattern: 3, 4

1. Hap - py hol - i - day, _____ hap - py hol - i - day. _____ While the / May the

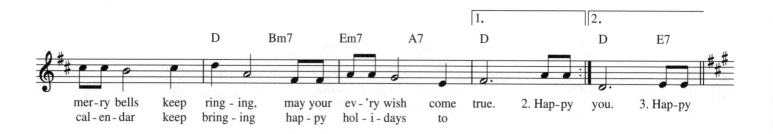

mer - ry bells keep ring - ing, may your ev - 'ry wish come true. 2. Hap-py you. 3. Hap-py
cal - en - dar keep bring - ing hap - py hol - i - days to

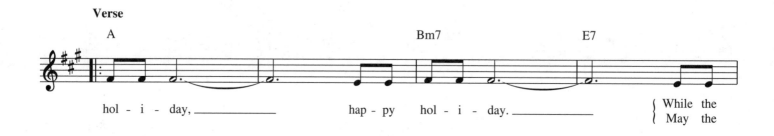

hol - i - day, _____ hap - py hol - i - day. _____ While the / May the

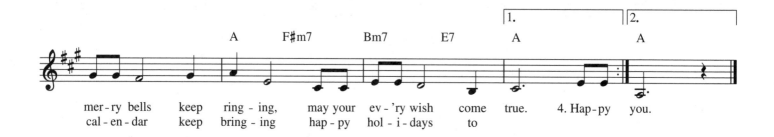

mer - ry bells keep ring - ing, may your ev - 'ry wish come true. 4. Hap-py you.
cal - en - dar keep bring - ing hap - py hol - i - days to

© Copyright 1941, 1942 by Irving Berlin
Copyright Renewed
International Copyright Secured   All Rights Reserved

Here Comes Santa Claus
(Right Down Santa Claus Lane)

Words and Music by Gene Autry and Oakley Haldeman

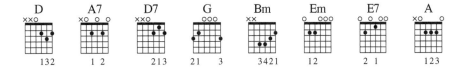

Strum Pattern: 3
Pick Pattern: 3

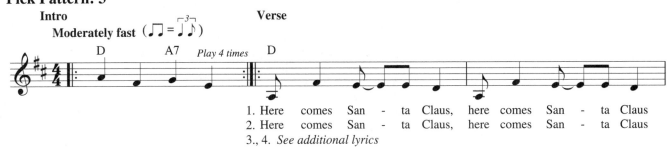

1. Here comes San - ta Claus, here comes San - ta Claus
2. Here comes San - ta Claus, here comes San - ta Claus
3., 4. *See additional lyrics*

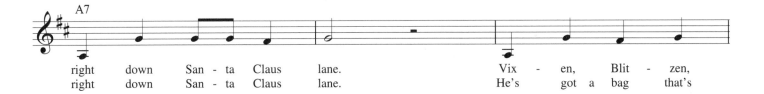

right down San - ta Claus lane. Vix - en, Blit - zen,
right down San - ta Claus lane. He's got a bag that's

all of his rein - deer pull - ing all ____ the reins. ____
filled ____ with toys for boys and girls a - gain. ____

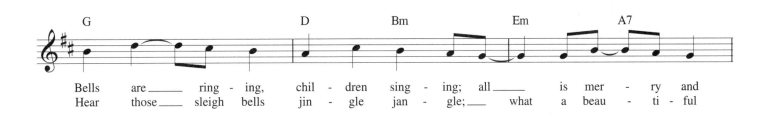

Bells are ____ ring - ing, chil - dren sing - ing; all ____ is mer - ry and
Hear those ____ sleigh bells jin - gle jan - gle; ____ what a beau - ti - ful

bright. Hang your stock - ings and say your prayers, ___ 'cause San -
sight. Jump in bed and cov - er up your head, 'cause San -

© 1947 (Renewed) Gene Autry's Western Music Publishing Co.
All Rights Reserved   Used by Permission

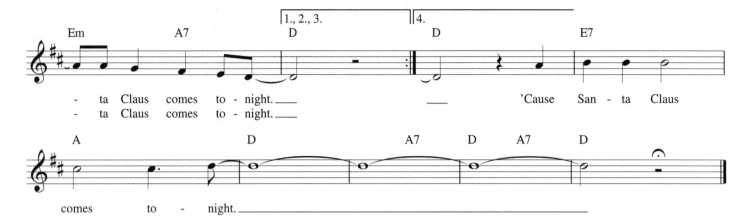

-ta Claus comes to - night.____
-ta Claus comes to - night.____ ____ 'Cause San - ta Claus

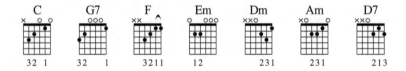

comes to - night. ____

Additional Lyrics

3. Here comes Santa Claus, here comes Santa Claus
   Right down Santa Claus lane.
   He doesn't care if you're rich or poor,
   For he loves you just the same.
   Santa knows that we're God's children;
   That makes ev'rything right.
   Fill your hearts with Christmas cheer
   'Cause Santa Claus comes tonight.

4. Here comes Santa Claus, here comes Santa Claus
   Right down Santa Claus lane.
   He'll come around when the chimes ring out;
   It's Christmas morn again.
   Peace on earth will come to all
   If we just follow the Light.
   Let's give thanks to the Lord above,
   'Cause Santa Claus comes tonight.

A Holly Jolly Christmas

Music and Lyrics by Johnny Marks

Strum Pattern: 2, 3
Pick Pattern: 3, 4

1. Have a (4.) hol - ly jol - ly Christ - mas, it's the best time of the year.

I don't know if there'll be snow but have a cup of cheer. 2., 5. Have a

Copyright © 1962, 1964 (Renewed 1990, 1992) St. Nicholas Music Inc., 1619 Broadway, New York, New York 10019
All Rights Reserved

Verse

hol - ly jol - ly Christ - mas, and when you walk down the street,

say hel - lo to friends you know and ev - 'ry - one you meet.

Bridge

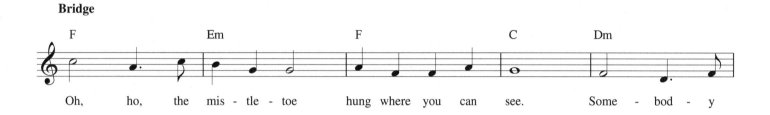

Oh, ho, the mis - tle - toe hung where you can see. Some - bod - y

Verse

waits for you, kiss her once for me. 3., 6. Have a hol - ly jol - ly Christ - mas, and in

case you did - n't hear, oh, by gol - ly, have a hol - ly jol - ly Christ - mas this

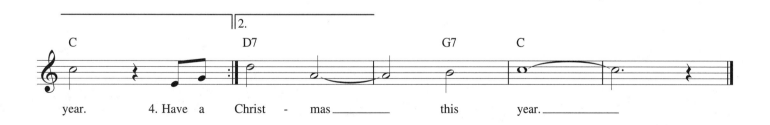

year. 4. Have a Christ - mas_____ this year._____

Happy Xmas
(War Is Over)

Words and Music by John Lennon and Yoko Ono

Strum Pattern: 8
Pick Pattern: 8

© 1971 (Renewed 1999) LENONO.MUSIC and ONO MUSIC
All Rights Controlled and Administered by EMI BLACKWOOD MUSIC INC.
All Rights Reserved   International Copyright Secured   Used by Permission

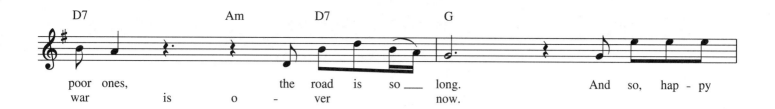

D7   Am   D7   G

poor ones,   the road is so ___ long.   And so, hap - py
war   is   o - ver   now.

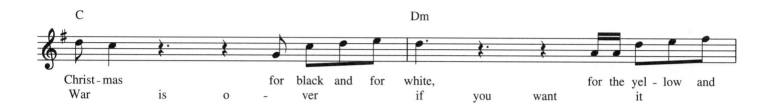

C   Dm

Christ - mas   for black and for white,   for the yel - low and
War   is   o - ver   if   you   want   it

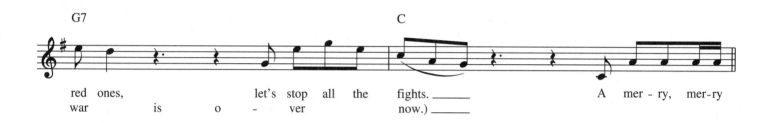

G7   C

red ones,   let's stop all the fights. _____   A mer - ry, mer - ry
war   is   o - ver   now.) _____

Chorus

F   G

Christ - mas   and a hap - py new year,   let's hope it's a

D.S. al Coda

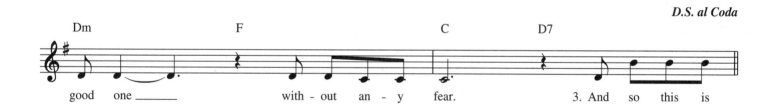

Dm   F   C   D7

good one _____   with - out an - y fear.   3. And so this is

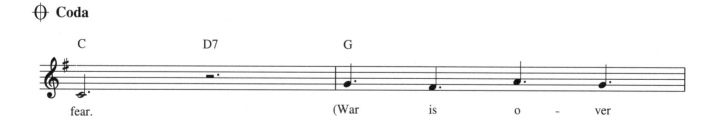

⊕ **Coda**

C   D7   G

fear.   (War   is   o - ver

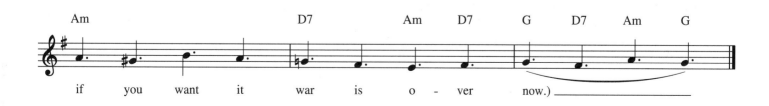

Am   D7   Am D7   G   D7 Am   G

if   you   want   it   war   is   o - ver   now.) _____

Holly Leaves and Christmas Trees

Words and Music by Red West and Glen Spreen

Strum Pattern: 2
Pick Pattern: 4

Verse
Moderately slow

Some-where in, _____ in the dis-tant night _____ I _____ hear

Christ-mas bells. _____ The gen-tle snow _____ keeps fall-ing down _____ on

peo-ple _____ who are home-ward bound. _____ That's the way _____ it's

al-ways been; _____ the cir-cle _____ nev-er real-ly ends. _____

Christ-mas seems _____ to come and go, _____ home's a place _____ that _____

Chorus

I don't know. _____ Hol-ly leaves _____ and Christ-mas trees, _____

it's that time _____ of year. _____ Lights a-glow _____ and mis-tle-toe _____ don't

Copyright © 1971 (Renewed) by Elvis Presley Music
All Rights Administered by Cherry River Music Co. and Chrysalis Songs
International Copyright Secured   All Rights Reserved

mean a thing___ when you're not here.   As I walk,___ walk this lone-ly street,___ the

sound of snow___ be - neath my feet,___ I think of how,___ how it

used to be ___ when hol - ly leaves___ and Christ-mas trees ___

used to mean ___ so much to me. ___

(There's No Place Like)
Home for the Holidays

Words by Al Stillman
Music by Robert Allen

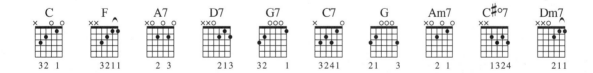

Strum Pattern: 3
Pick Pattern: 3

Oh, there's   no   place like   home   for the   hol - i - days,___   'cause no

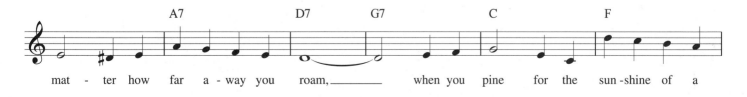

mat - ter how   far a - way   you   roam,___   when you   pine   for the   sun - shine of a

© Copyright 1954 Roncom Music Co.
Copyright Renewed 1982 and Assigned to Charlie Deitcher Productions, Inc. and Kitty Anne Music Co.
International Copyright Secured   All Rights Reserved

How Lovely Is Christmas

Words by Arnold Sundgaard
Music by Alec Wilder

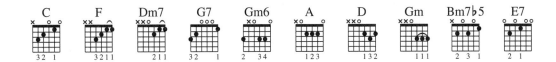

Strum Pattern: 7
Pick Pattern: 7

Verse

Moderately

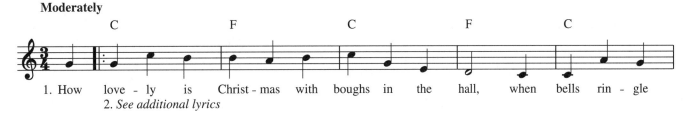

1. How love - ly is Christ - mas with boughs in the hall, when bells rin - gle
2. *See additional lyrics*

jin - gle and friends come to call. How love - ly is Christ - mas with

joy on the wing, while un - der your win - dow the car - ol - ers

sing: "God rest ye; be mer - ry; give peace where you may; re -

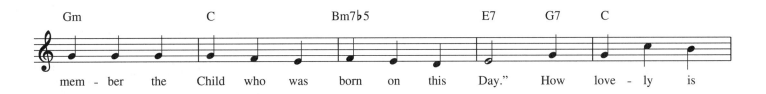

mem - ber the Child who was born on this Day." How love - ly is

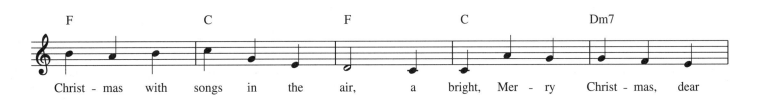

Christ - mas with songs in the air, a bright, Mer - ry Christ - mas, dear

TRO - © Copyright 1957 (Renewed) Ludlow Music, Inc., New York, NY
International Copyright Secured
All Rights Reserved Including Public Performance For Profit
Used by Permission

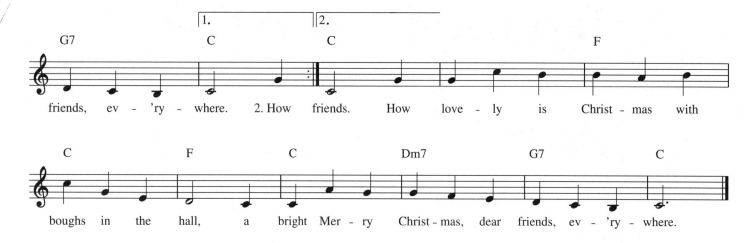

friends, ev - 'ry - where. 2. How friends. How love - ly is Christ - mas with boughs in the hall, a bright Mer - ry Christ - mas, dear friends, ev - 'ry - where.

Additional Lyrics

2. How lovely is Christmas when children are near,
   The sound of their laughter, sweet season of cheer.
   How lovely is Christmas with gifts by the tree,
   Each gift tells a story, oh, what will it be.
   The Yule Log is burning, the stars gleam above;
   Remember the gift of the Christ Child is love.
   The bells ring for Christmas, our story now ends.
   Goodnight, Merry Christmas, dear neighbors and friends.
   How lovely is Christmas with boughs in the hall,
   A bright Merry Christmas, dear friends, ev'rywhere.

I Still Believe in Santa Claus

Words and Music by Maurice Starr and Al Lancellotti

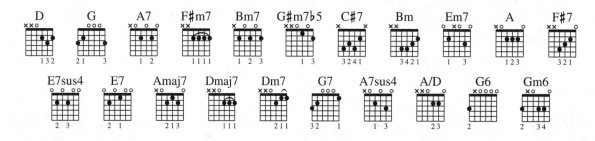

*Strum Pattern: 4
*Pick Pattern: 3

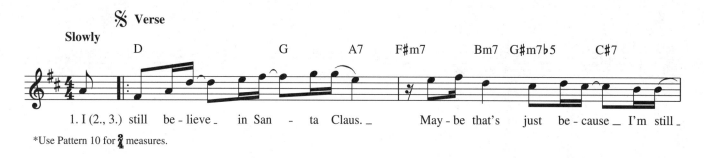

1. I (2., 3.) still be - lieve _ in San - ta Claus. _ May - be that's just be - cause _ I'm still

*Use Pattern 10 for 2/4 measures.

_____ a child _ at heart. And I

© 1989 EMI APRIL MUSIC INC., MAURICE STARR MUSIC and AL LANCELLOTTI MUSIC
All Rights for MAURICE STARR MUSIC Controlled and Administered by EMI APRIL MUSIC INC.
All Rights Reserved   International Copyright Secured   Used by Permission

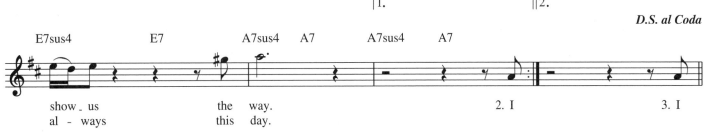

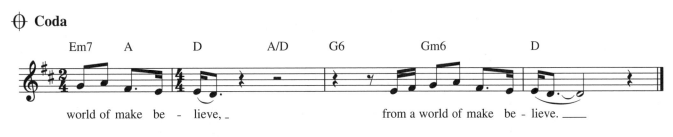

I Heard the Bells on Christmas Day

Words by Henry Wadsworth Longfellow
Adapted by Johnny Marks
Music by Johnny Marks

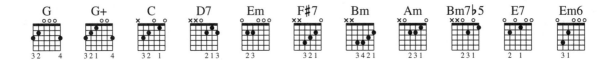

Strum Pattern: 4
Pick Pattern: 5

Verse
Moderately

1. I heard the bells on Christ-mas Day, their old fa-mil-iar car-ols play; and
2., 3. *See additional lyrics*

wild and sweet the words re-peat, of peace on earth good will to men. I

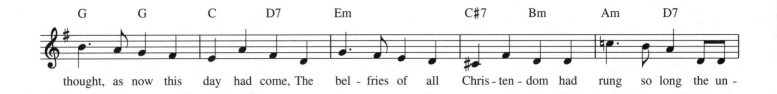

thought, as now this day had come, The bel-fries of all Chris-ten-dom had rung so long the un-

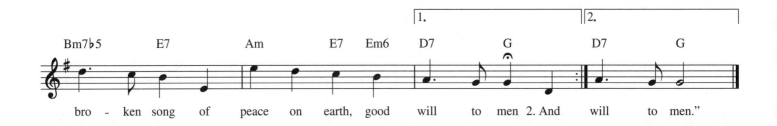

bro-ken song of peace on earth, good will to men 2. And will to men."

Additional Lyrics

2. And in despair I bowed my head;
   "There is no peace on earth," I said,
   "For hate is strong, and mocks the song
   Of peace on earth, good will to men."
   Then pealed the bells more loud and deep;
   "God is not dead, no noth He sleep.
   The wrong shall fail, the right prevail
   With peace on earth good will to men."

Copyright © 1956 (Renewed 1984) St. Nicholas Music Inc., 1619 Broadway, New York, New York 10019
All Rights Reserved

I Saw Mommy Kissing Santa Claus

Words and Music by Tommie Connor

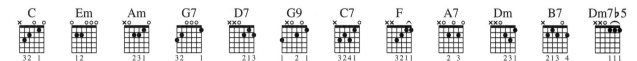

Strum Pattern: 2, 3
Pick Pattern: 3, 4

Verse
Moderately

I saw Mom-my kiss-ing San - ta Claus, un-der-neath the mis-tle-toe last

night. _____ She did - n't see me creep down the stairs to have a peep. She

thought that I was tucked up in my bed-room fast a - sleep. Then I saw

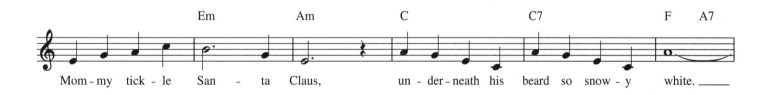

Mom-my tick - le San - ta Claus, un-der-neath his beard so snow-y white. _____

___ Oh, what a laugh it would have been, if Dad-dy had on - ly seen Mom-my

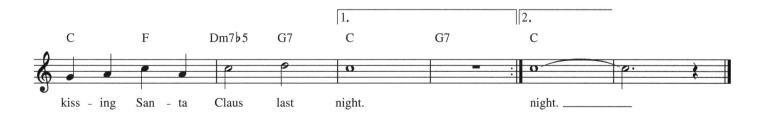

kiss-ing San - ta Claus last night. night. _____

Copyright © 1952 by Regent Music Corporation (BMI)
Copyright Renewed by Jewel Music Publishing Co., Inc. (ASCAP)
International Copyright Secured   All Rights Reserved
Used by Permission

I'll Be Home for Christmas

Words and Music by Kim Gannon and Walter Kent

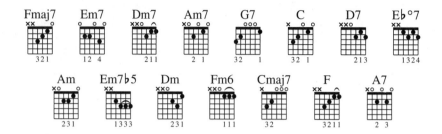

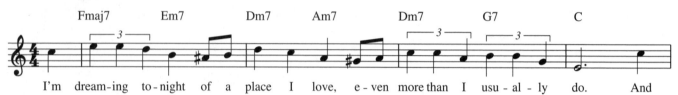

Strum Pattern: 4, 3
Pick Pattern: 4, 3

© Copyright 1943 by Gannon & Kent Music Co., Inc., Beverly Hills, CA
Copyright Renewed
International Copyright Secured   All Rights Reserved

I'm Spending Christmas With You

Words and Music by Tom Occhipinti

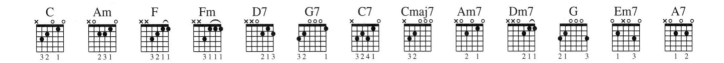

Strum Pattern: 7
Pick Pattern: 7

Verse
Moderately slow

1. The snow is gen-tly fall-ing, the night is so cold. _ The moon shines _ on the
2. *See additional lyrics*

snow cov-ered trees. The road seemed like ____ for-ev-er, ____ but I'm

fi-nal-ly home. _ We're a-lone on this Christ-mas Eve.

𝄋 Chorus

I'm spend-ing Christ-mas ____ with ___ you. ____ 'Tis the

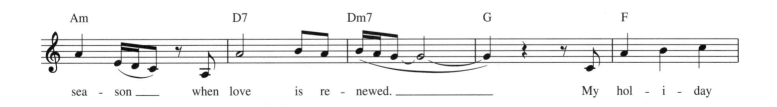

sea-son ___ when love is re-newed. ____ My hol-i-day

Copyright © 1981 Sony/ATV Songs LLC
All Rights Administered by Sony/ATV Music Publishing, 8 Music Square West, Nashville, TN 37203
International Copyright Secured   All Rights Reserved

To Coda

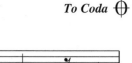

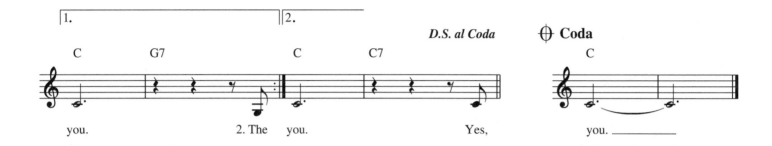

Additional Lyrics

2. The fireplace is burning and your hands feel so warm.
We're hanging popcorn on the tree.
I take you in my arms, your lips touch mine.
It feels like our first Christmas Eve.

It's Beginning to Look Like Christmas

By Meredith Willson

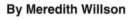

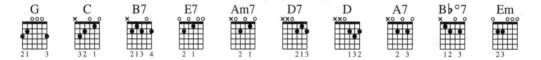

Strum Pattern: 2, 3
Pick Pattern: 3, 4

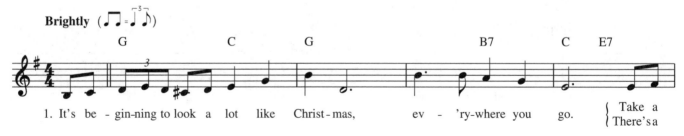

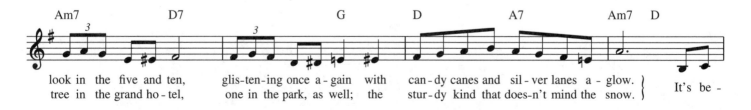

© 1951 PLYMOUTH MUSIC CO., INC.
© Renewed 1979 FRANK MUSIC CORP. and MEREDITH WILLSON MUSIC
All Rights Reserved

gin - ning to look a lot like Christ - mas,

{ toys in ev - 'ry store. But the
soon the bells will start. And the

To Coda ⊕

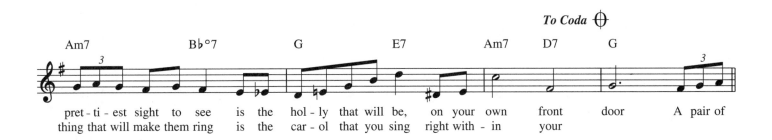

pret - ti - est sight to see is the hol - ly that will be, on your own front door A pair of
thing that will make them ring is the car - ol that you sing right with - in your

Bridge

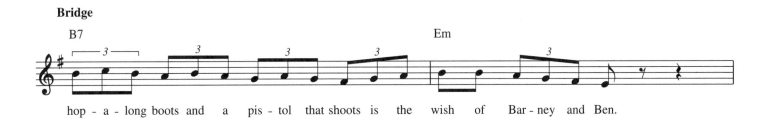

hop - a - long boots and a pis - tol that shoots is the wish of Bar - ney and Ben.

Dolls that will talk and will go for a walk is the hope of Jan - ice and Jen. And

⊕ **Coda**

D.S. al Coda

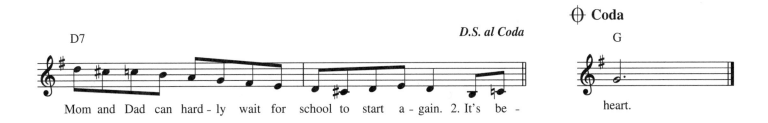

Mom and Dad can hard - ly wait for school to start a - gain. 2. It's be -

heart.

I'll Be Home on Christmas Day

Words and Music by Michael Jarrett

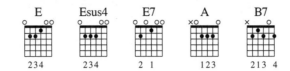

Strum Pattern: 3
Pick Pattern: 3

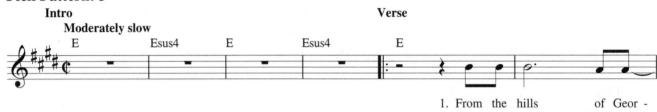

Intro   Verse

Moderately slow

1. From the hills   of Geor -
2. It's been so   man - y
3. There were times I'd think a - bout

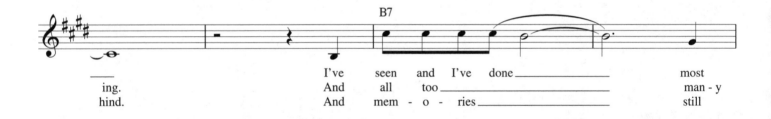

- gia,   a - cross the plains   of Ten - nes - see,
___ times be - fore   she left that can - dle burn -
___ her,   all the love I _____ left be -

___ ing.   I've seen and I've done _____ most
ing.   And all too _____ man - y
hind.   And mem - o - ries _____ still

ev - 'ry - thing   that a man can _____ do or
tears that fell,   my soul _____ filled with
lin - ger   with - in my _____ trou - bled

see.   But if I _____ could on - ly
yearn - ing.   If I had _____ an - y sense
mind.   If I could _____ set a - side

Copyright © 1971 (Renewed) by Elvis Presley Music
All Rights Administered by Cherry River Music Co. and Chrysalis Songs
International Copyright Secured   All Rights Reserved

I've Got My Love to Keep Me Warm

from the 20th Century Fox Motion Picture ON THE AVENUE
Words and Music by Irving Berlin

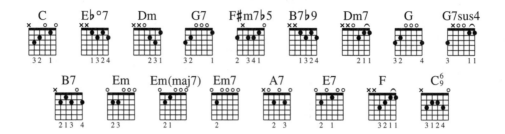

Strum Pattern: 3, 4
Pick Pattern: 3, 4

Verse

Brightly

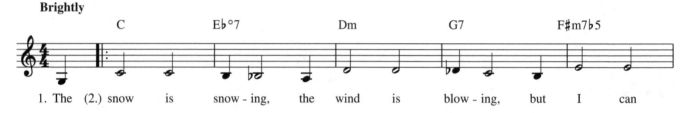

1. The (2.) snow is snow-ing, the wind is blow-ing, but I can

weath-er the storm. ___ What do I care how much it may storm? ___

___ I've got my love to keep me warm.

I can't re-mem-ber a worse De-cem-ber; just

© Copyright 1936, 1937 by Irving Berlin
© Arrangement Copyright 1948 by Irving Berlin
Copyright Renewed
International Copyright Secured   All Rights Reserved

watch those i - ci - cles form. _____ What do I care if

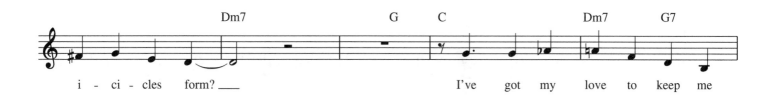

i - ci - cles form? _____ I've got my love to keep me

Bridge

warm. Off with my o - ver - coat, _ off with my

glove. I need no o - ver - coat, _ I'm burn - ing with love. My

Outro-Verse

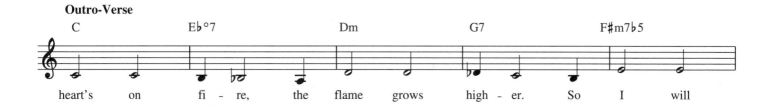

heart's on fi - re, the flame grows high - er. So I will

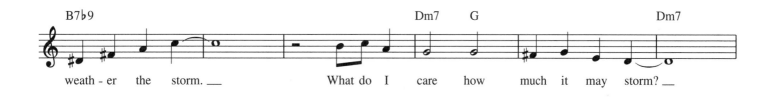

weath - er the storm. _ What do I care how much it may storm? _

I've got my love to keep me warm. 2. The warm. _____

It Must Have Been the Mistletoe
(Our First Christmas)

By Justin Wilde and Doug Konecky

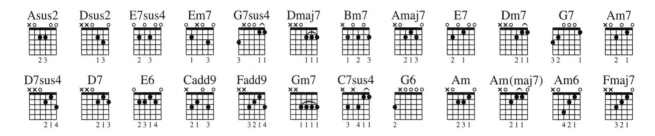

Strum Pattern: 8
Pick Pattern: 8

Verse
Moderately

1. It must have been __ the mis-tle-toe, __ the la-zy fire, __ the fall-ing snow, __ the

mag - ic in ____ the frost-y air, ____ that feel - ing ev - 'ry-where. It

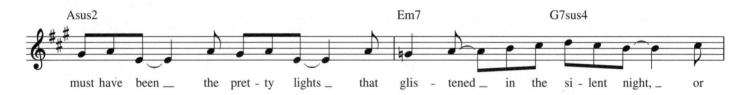

must have been __ the pret-ty lights __ that glis - tened __ in the si - lent night, __ or

may - be just ____ the stars so bright __ that shined a - bove you.

Bridge

Our first Christ - mas, more than __ we'd been dream - ing of.

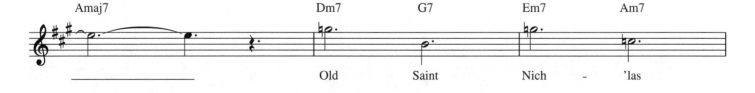

_____ Old Saint Nich - 'las

© Copyright 1979 Songcastle Music (ASCAP) and Cat's Whiskers Music (ASCAP)/both admin. by ICG
All Rights Reserved   Used by Permission

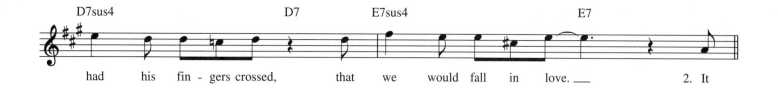

D7sus4   D7   E7sus4   E7

had   his   fin - gers crossed,   that   we   would   fall   in   love. __   2. It

Verse

Asus2

could have been __   the   hol - i - day, __   the   mid-night   ride __   up - on   a   sleigh, _   the

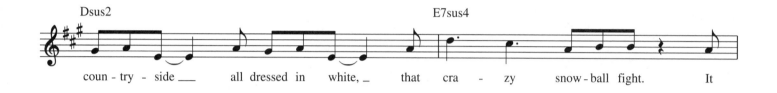

Dsus2   E7sus4

coun - try - side __   all   dressed   in   white, _   that   cra - zy   snow - ball   fight.   It

Asus2   Em7   G7sus4

could have been __   the   stee - ple   bell __   that   wrapped   us   up   with - in   it's   spell. __   It

Dmaj7   Bm7   E7sus4   E6

on - ly   took   one   kiss   to   know, __   it   must   have   been   the

Bridge

Asus2   Dmaj7   Amaj7

mis - tle - toe.   Our   first   Christ -   mas,

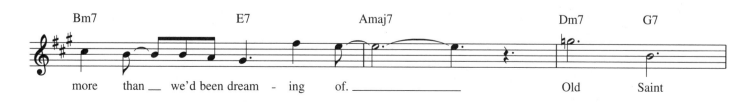

Bm7   E7   Amaj7   Dm7   G7

more   than __   we'd been   dream - ing   of. _____   Old   Saint

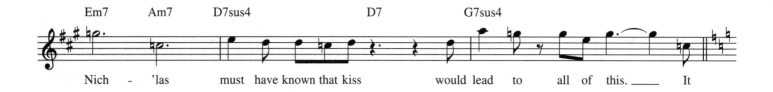

Em7   Am7   D7sus4   D7   G7sus4

Nich - 'las   must   have   known   that   kiss   would   lead   to   all   of   this. _____ It

Outro

Cadd9

must   have   been __ the   mis - tle - toe, ___ the   la - zy   fire, ___ the   fall - ing   snow, _ the

Fadd9   G7sus4

mag - ic   in ____ the   frost - y   air, ____ that   made   me   love   you.   On

Cadd9   Gm7   C7sus4

Christ - mas Eve ___ a   wish come true, _ that   night   I ____ fell   in   love   with   you. __ It

Fadd9   Dm7   G7sus4

on - ly   took ___ one   kiss   to   know, _ it   must   have   been   the

Cadd9   Dm7   G6   Am   Am(maj7) Am7   Am6

mis - tle - toe!   It   must   have   been   the   mis - tle - toe!   It

Dm7   G7sus4   Cadd9   Fmaj7   Cadd9

must   have   been   the   mis - tle - toe!

It's Christmas Time All Over the World

Words and Music by Hugh Martin

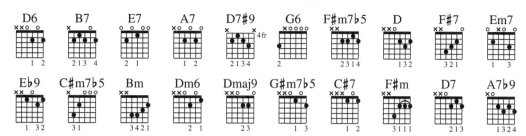

Strum Pattern: 4
Pick Pattern: 3

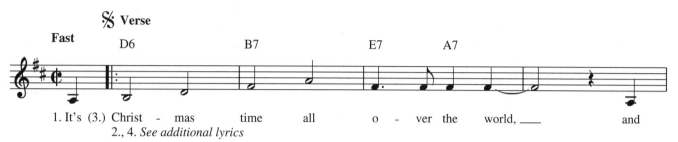

It's (3.) Christ - mas time all o - ver the world, and
2., 4. *See additional lyrics*

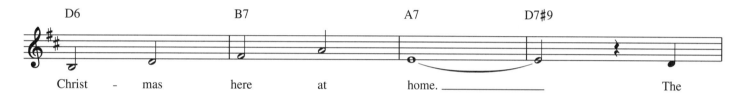

Christ - mas here at home. The

church bells chime wher - ev - er we roam, so

Joy - eux No - ël, Fe - liz Na - tal,
(Zhwah - yuh No - el) *(Feh - leez Nah - tahl)*

Gel - luk - kig Kerst - feest to you!
(Huh - lukh - kuh Kairst - feest)

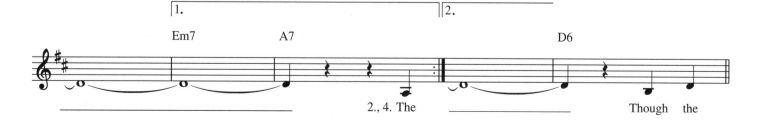

2., 4. The Though the

TRO - © Copyright 1965 (Renewed) Cromwell Music, Inc., New York, NY
International Copyright Secured
All Rights Reserved Including Public Performance For Profit
Used by Permission

83

Bridge

cus - toms _____ may change, _____ and the lan - guage _____

_____ is strange, _____ this ap - peal we feel is

real in Hol - land or Hong _____ Kong. _____ It's

Outro

Christ - mas time all o - ver the world, _____ in

plac - es near and far; _____ and so, my

friends, wher - ev - er you are, _____ a Fröh - li - che Weih -
(Fruh - lee - kheh Vy -

nacht - en! Ka - la Christ - ou - ge - na! Yo - i Kurisu -
nakh - ten) (Kah - lah Hrees - too - yeh-nah) (Yo - ee Kreess -

To Coda

ma - su! Which means a ver - y mer - ry Christ - mas
mah - soo)

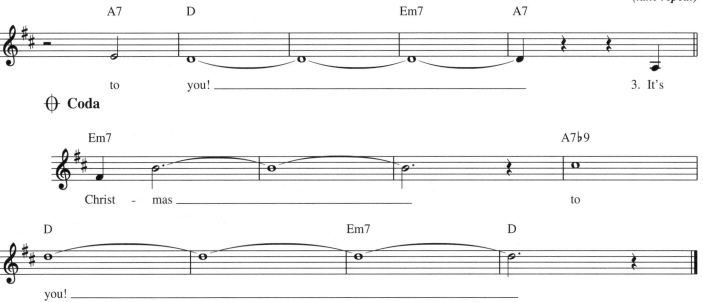

to you! _____ 3. It's

Coda

Christ - mas _____ to

you! _____

Additional Lyrics

2., 4. The snow is thick in most of the world
And children's eyes are wide
As old Saint Nick gets ready to ride,
So Feliz Navidad, Craciun Fericit,
(Feh-lees Nah-vee-dahd) (Krah-choon Feeh-ree-cheet)
And Happy New Year to you!

Jesus Is Born

Words and Music by Steve Green, Phil Naish and Colleen Green

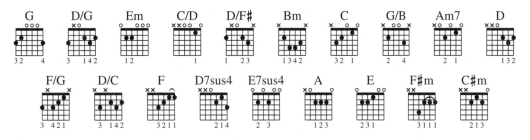

*Strum Pattern: 2
*Pick Pattern: 4

Intro
Moderately fast

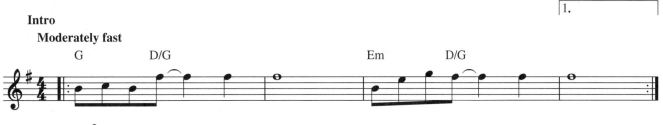

*Use Pattern 10 for ⅜ measures.

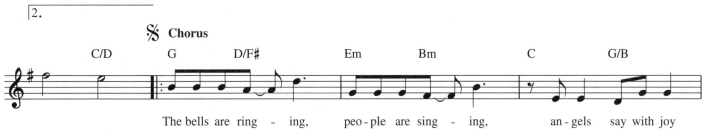

The bells are ring - ing, peo - ple are sing - ing, an - gels say with joy

© 1987 BIRDWING MUSIC, PAMELA KAY MUSIC, BECKENGUS MUSIC and BMG SONGS, INC.
BIRDWING MUSIC, PAMELA KAY MUSIC and BECKENGUS MUSIC Admin. by EMI CHRISTIAN MUSIC PUBLISHING
All Rights Reserved   Used by Permission

4th time, To Coda ⊕

"Je - sus is born!" There in a man - ger, He was no stran - ger. Pro-phe-sied, now a - live,

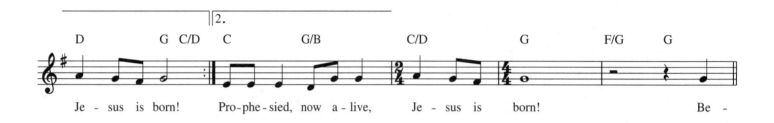

Je - sus is born! Pro-phe-sied, now a - live, Je - sus is born! Be -

Bridge

hold the gift of sal - va - tion, a light for ___ all to see, re -

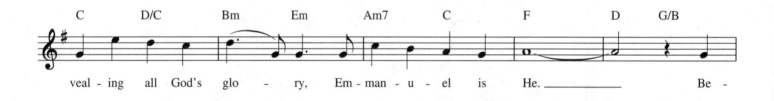

veal - ing all God's glo - ry, Em - man - u - el is He. _____ Be -

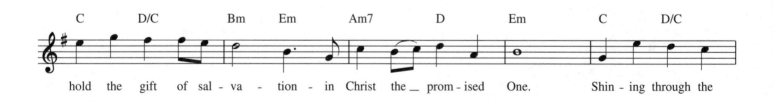

hold the gift of sal - va - tion - in Christ the ___ prom - ised One. Shin - ing through the

D.S. al Coda
(take repeat)

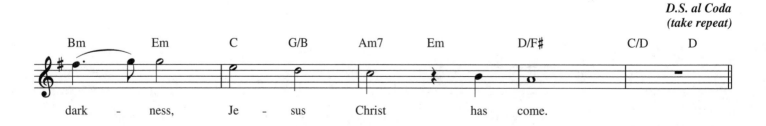

dark - ness, Je - sus Christ has come.

⊕ Coda

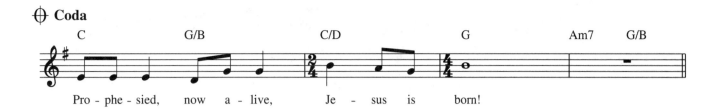

Pro - phe - sied, now a - live, Je - sus is born!

Bridge

Glo - ry to ___ the King, Lord of ev - 'ry - thing, Christ has fi - nal - ly come.

Glo - ry to ___ the King, let the peo - ple sing Hal - le - lu - jah, _____

Outro-Chorus

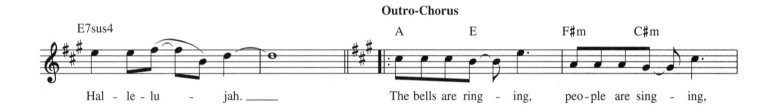

Hal - le - lu - jah. _____ The bells are ring - ing, peo - ple are sing - ing,

an - gels say with joy, "Je - sus is born!" There in a man - ger, He was no stran - ger.

Glo - ri - fied, still a - live, Je - sus is born! Je - sus is born! Glo - ri - fied, still a - live,

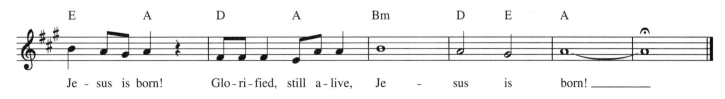

Je - sus is born! Glo - ri - fied, still a - live, Je - sus is born! _____

It Won't Seem Like Christmas
(Without You)

Words and Music by J.A. Balthrop

Strum Pattern: 9
Pick Pattern: 7

Copyright © 1966 (Renewed), 1971 (Renewed) by Elvis Presley Music
All Rights Administered by Cherry River Music Co. and Chrysalis Songs
International Copyright Secured   All Rights Reserved

just a - bout _____ to this time of year. ____ Looks like

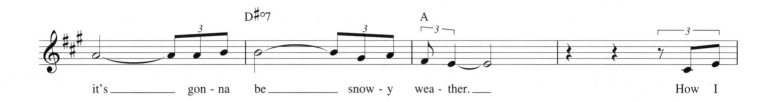

it's _____ gon - na be _____ snow - y wea - ther. ____ How I

wish that you could be here. ____ But it

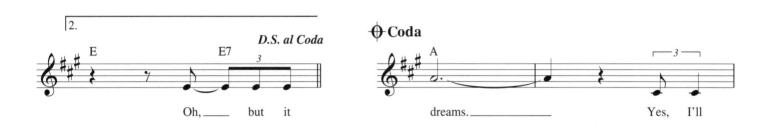

Oh, ____ but it   dreams. _____ Yes, I'll

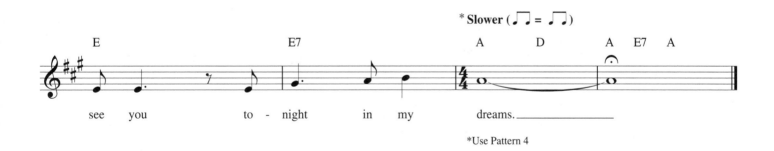

see you to - night in my dreams. _____

*Use Pattern 4

Additional Lyrics

2. In the distance I hear sleigh bells ringing.
   The holly's so pretty this year;
   And the carol that somebody's singing
   Reminds me of our Christmas last year.

It's Christmas in New York

Words and Music by Billy Butt

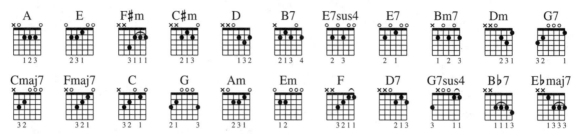

Strum Pattern: 4
Pick Pattern: 3

Verse

Moderately

1., 2. Church-bells are ring - ing, ___ choirs ___ are sing - ing, ___

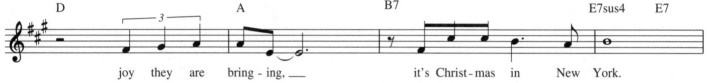

joy they are bring - ing, ___ it's Christ-mas in New York.

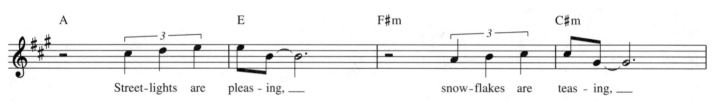

Street-lights are pleas - ing, ___ snow-flakes are teas - ing, ___

Cen - tral Park's freez - ing, ___ it's Christ-mas in ___ New ___ York. The

Bridge

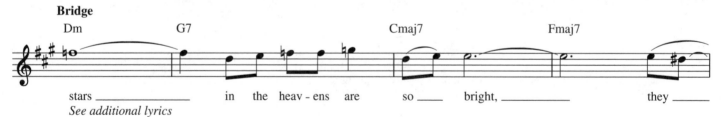

stars ___ in the heav - ens are so ___ bright, ___ they ___
See additional lyrics

___ tell ___ of a ba - by that was born ___ on this night.

Verse

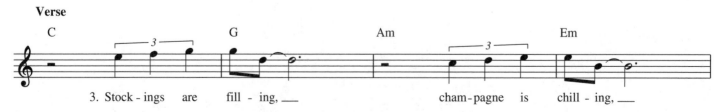

3. Stock - ings are fill - ing, ___ cham-pagne is chill - ing, ___

Copyright © 1986 by Billybee Songs and Misty Music AB, Stockholm, Sweden
Administered in the United States and Canada by Galahad Music, Inc.
International Copyright Secured All Rights Reserved

Additional Lyrics

2. Rest'rant signs swaying, blue skies are graying,
Ev'ryone saying, it's Christmas in New York.
Skyscrapers gleaming, Broadway lights beaming,
Children are dreaming, it's Christmas in New York.

Bridge The lights on the Christmas tree are fine,
The sights of shopping sprees, the gifts, yours and mine.

Jingle-Bell Rock

Words and Music by Joe Beal and Jim Boothe

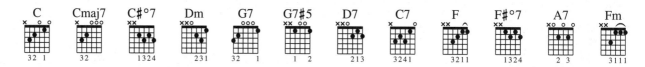

Strum Pattern: 1, 3
Pick Pattern: 2, 3

Verse
Moderate Rock

1., 2. Jin-gle-bell, jin-gle-bell, jin-gle-bell rock, jin-gle-bell swing and jin-gle-bells ring.

Snow-in' and blow-in' up bush-els of fun, now the jin-gle-hop has be-gun.

Jin-gle-bell, jin-gle-bell, jin-gle-bell rock, jin-gle-bells chime in jin-gle-bell time.

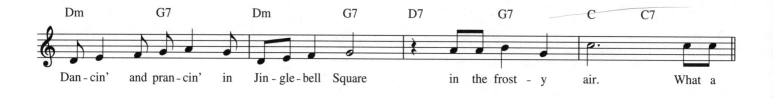

Dan-cin' and pran-cin' in Jin-gle-bell Square in the frost-y air. What a

Bridge

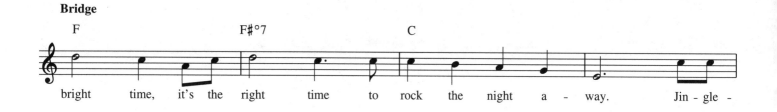

bright time, it's the right time to rock the night a-way. Jin-gle-

bell time is a swell time to go glid-in' in a one horse sleigh.

Copyright © 1957 by Chappell & Co.
Copyright Renewed
International Copyright Secured   All Rights Reserved

Outro

Gid-dy-up, jin-gle horse pick up your feet, jin-gle a-round the clock.

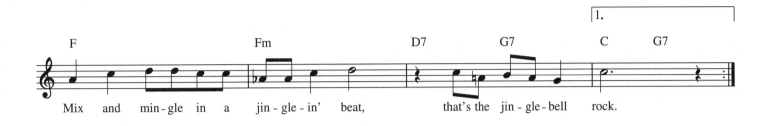

Mix and min-gle in a jin-gle-in' beat, that's the jin-gle-bell rock.

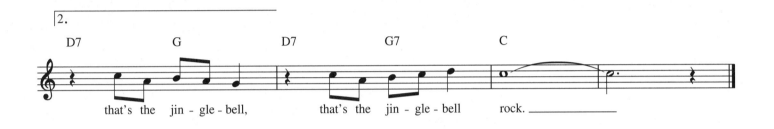

that's the jin-gle-bell, that's the jin-gle-bell rock. _____

A Marshmallow World

Words by Carl Sigman
Music by Peter De Rose

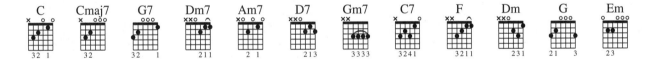

Strum Pattern: 3
Pick Pattern: 3

Intro
Brightly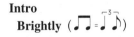

1. It's a

%. Verse

(4.) marsh-mal-low world in the win-ter when the snow comes to cov-er the ground. It's the
marsh-mal-low clouds be-ing friend-ly in the arms of ev-er-green trees. And the

Copyright © 1949, 1950 Shapiro, Bernstein & Co., Inc., New York
Copyright Renewed
International Copyright Secured   All Rights Reserved
Used by Permission

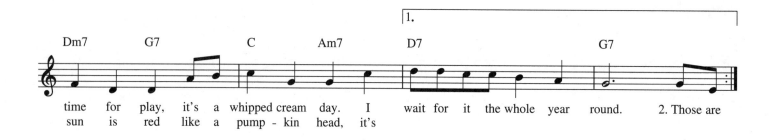

time for play, it's a whipped cream day. I wait for it the whole year round. 2. Those are
sun is red like a pump - kin head, it's

To Coda

Chorus

shin - ing so your nose won't freeze. The world is your snow ball; see how it grows.

That's how it goes, when - ev - er it snows. The world is your snow ball; just for a song, get

Verse

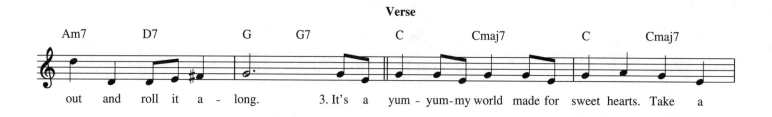

out and roll it a - long. 3. It's a yum - yum-my world made for sweet hearts. Take a

walk with your fa - vor - ite girl. It's a sug - ar date. What if spring is late? In

D.S. al Coda
(take repeat)

✛ **Coda**

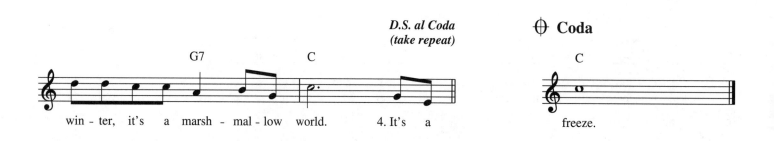

win - ter, it's a marsh - mal - low world. 4. It's a   freeze.

The Last Month of the Year
(What Month Was Jesus Born In?)

Words and Music by Vera Hall
Adapted and Arranged by Ruby Pickens Tartt and Alan Lomax

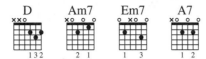

Strum Pattern: 6
Pick Pattern: 3

Verse

Moderately

1. What month was my Je-sus born in? Last month of the year!
2., 3., 4 *See additional lyrics*

What month was my Je-sus born in? Last month of the year! Oh,

Chorus

Jan-u-ar-y, Feb-ru-ar-y, March,

A-pril, May, June, O Lord, You got Ju-ly, Au-gust, Sep-tem-ber, Oc-

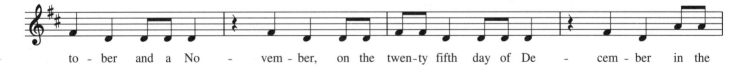

to-ber and a No-vem-ber, on the twen-ty fifth day of De-cem-ber in the

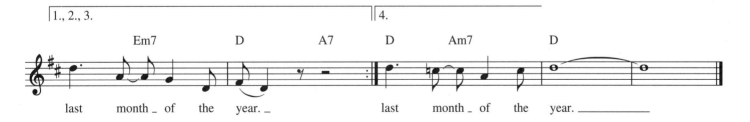

last month of the year. last month of the year.

Additional Lyrics

2. Well, they laid Him in the manger,
   Last month of the year!
   Well, they laid Him in the manger,
   Last month of the year!

3. Wrapped Him up in swaddling clothing,
   Last month of the year!
   Wrapped Him up in swaddling clothing,
   Last month of the year!

4. He was born of the Virgin Mary,
   Last month of the year!
   He was born of the Virgin Mary,
   Last month of the year!

TRO - © Copyright 1960 (Renewed) Ludlow Music, Inc., New York, NY
International Copyright Secured
All Rights Reserved Including Public Performance For Profit
Used by Permission

Jingle, Jingle, Jingle

Music and Lyrics by Johnny Marks

Strum Pattern: 4
Pick Pattern: 4

Verse
Moderately

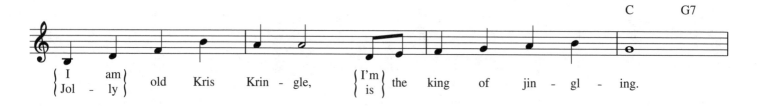

1., 2. Jin - gle, jin - gle, jin - gle, you will hear { my / his } sleigh bells ring.

{ I am / Jol - ly } old Kris Krin - gle, { I'm / is } the king of jin - gl - ing.

Jin - gle, jin - gle rein - deer, through the frost - y air they'll go.

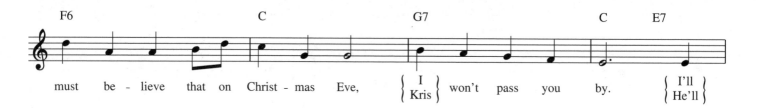

They are not just plain deer, they're the fast - est deer I know. You
Spoken: (Ho! Ho!)

must be - lieve that on Christ - mas Eve, { I / Kris } won't pass you by. { I'll / He'll }

dash a - way in { my / his } mag - ic sleigh, fly - ing through the sky.

Copyright © 1964 (Renewed 1992) St. Nicholas Music Inc., 1619 Broadway, New York, New York 10019
All Rights Reserved

Jin - gle, jin - gle rein - deer, through the frost - y air they'll go.

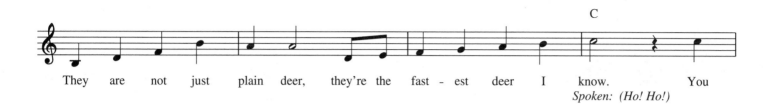

They are not just plain deer, they're the fast - est deer I know.   You
Spoken: (Ho! Ho!)

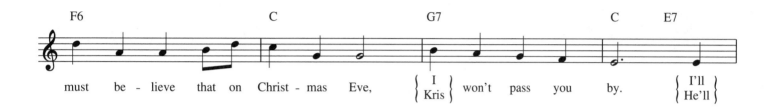

must be - lieve that on Christ - mas Eve, {I / Kris} won't pass you by.   {I'll / He'll}

dash a - way in {my / his} mag - ic sleigh, fly - ing through the sky.

Jin - gle, jin - gle, jin - gle, you will hear {my / his} sleigh bells ring.

1.

{ I am old Kris Krin - gle; I'm the king of jin - gl - ing.
Jol - ly old Kris Krin - gle is the
Spoken: (Ho! Ho!)

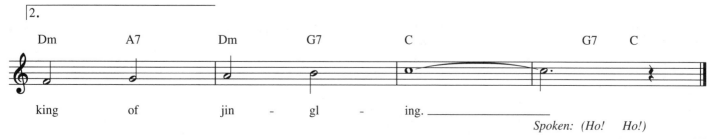

2.

king of jin - gl - ing. _____

Spoken: (Ho!   Ho!)

97

Let It Snow! Let It Snow! Let It Snow!

Words by Sammy Cahn
Music by Jule Styne

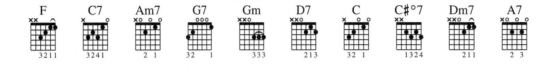

Strum Pattern: 2
Pick Pattern: 4

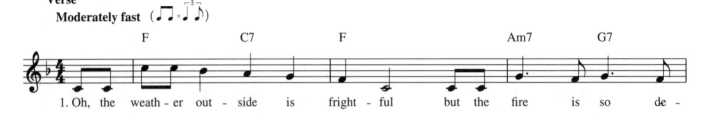

1. Oh, the weath-er out-side is fright-ful but the fire is so de-light-ful. And since we've no place to go, let it snow, let it snow, let it snow! 2. It

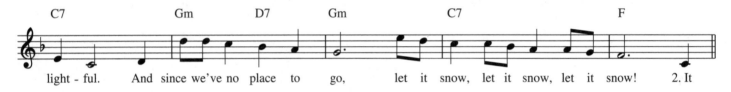

does-n't show signs of stop-ping, and I brought some corn for pop-ping. The
fire is slow-ly dy-ing and my dear, we're still good-bye-ing. But as

lights are turned way down low,
long as you love me so, let it snow, let it snow, let it snow! When we

fi-nal-ly kiss good-night, how I'll hate go-ing out in the storm. But if

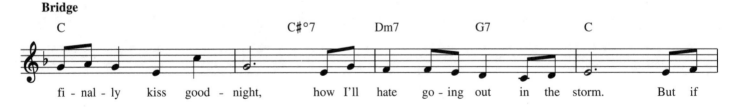

you'll real-ly hold me tight, all the way home I'll be warm. 3. The snow!

Copyright © 1945 by Producers Music Publishing Co. and Cahn Music Company
Copyright Renewed
All Rights for Producers Music Publishing Co. Administered by Chappell & Co.
All Rights for Cahn Music Company Administered by Cherry Lane Music Publishing Company, Inc. and DreamWorks Songs
International Copyright Secured   All Rights Reserved

The Merry Christmas Polka

Words by Paul Francis Webster
Music by Sonny Burke

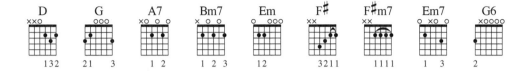

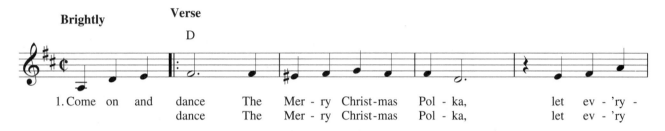

Strum Pattern: 4
Pick Pattern: 3

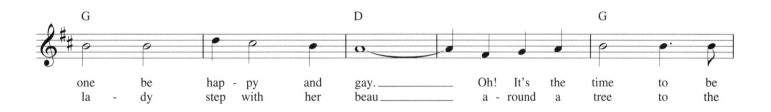

1. Come on and dance The Mer-ry Christ-mas Pol-ka, let ev-'ry-
   dance The Mer-ry Christ-mas Pol-ka, let ev-'ry

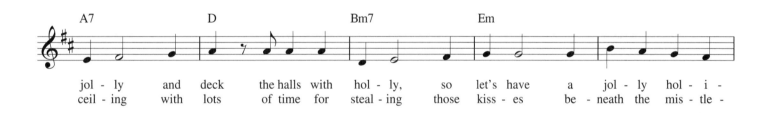

one be hap-py and gay. ___ Oh! It's the time to be
la - dy step with her beau ___ a-round a tree to the

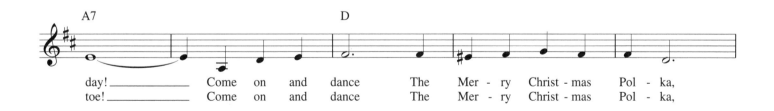

jol - ly and deck the halls with hol - ly, so let's have a jol-ly hol-i-
ceil - ing with lots of time for steal - ing those kiss - es be-neath the mis-tle-

day! ___ Come on and dance The Mer-ry Christ-mas Pol-ka,
toe! ___ Come on and dance The Mer-ry Christ-mas Pol-ka,

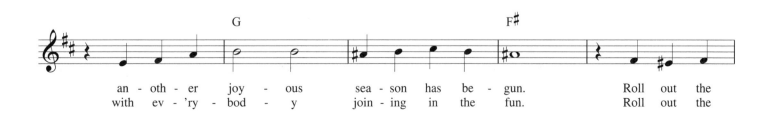

an - oth - er joy - ous sea - son has be - gun. Roll out the
with ev-'ry - bod - y join - ing in the fun. Roll out the

Copyright © 1949 by Alamo Music, Inc.
Copyright Renewed, Assigned to Chappell & Co. and Webster Music Co.
International Copyright Secured   All Rights Reserved

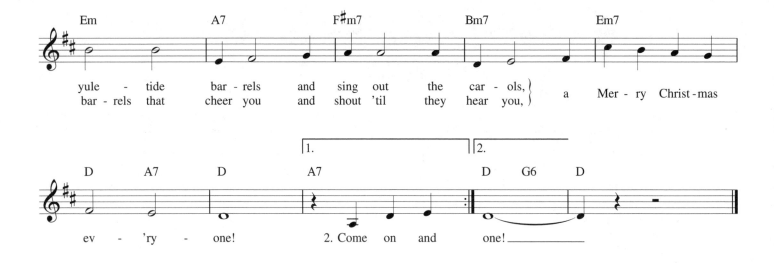

yule - tide   bar - rels   and   sing   out   the   car - ols,
bar - rels   that   cheer   you   and   shout   'til   they   hear   you,   a   Mer - ry   Christ - mas

ev - 'ry - one!   2. Come on and   one!

Merry Christmas, Baby

Words and Music by Lou Baxter and Johnny Moore

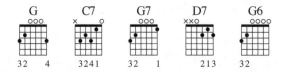

Strum Pattern: 1, 3
Pick Pattern: 4, 5

Verse
Moderate Blues

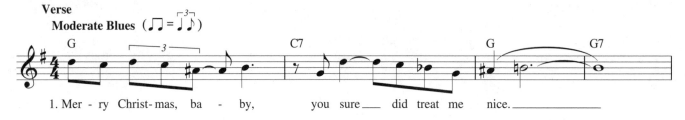

1. Mer - ry Christ - mas, ba - by,   you sure ___ did treat me nice. ___

Mer - ry Christ - mas ba - by,   you sure ___ did treat me nice. ___

___ Gave me a dia - mond ring for Christ - mas,   now I'm liv - in' in par - a - dise. ___

Copyright © 1948 by Unichappell Music, Inc.
Copyright Renewed
International Copyright Secured All Rights Reserved

Verse

2. Well, I'm feel - in' might - y fine, ___ got good mu - sic on my ra - di - o. ___

___ Well, I'm feel - in' might - y fine, ___ got good mu - sic on my ra - di - o. ___

___ Well, I want to kiss you, ba - by, while you're stand - in' 'neath the mis - tle - toe.

Outro-Verse

___ Saint Nick came down the chim - ney 'bout half - past three, ___ left

all these pret - ty pres - ents ___ that you see be - fore me. ___ Mer - ry Christ - mas, lit - tle ba - by,

you sure ___ been good to me. ___ I have - n't

had a drink this morn - in', ___ but I'm all lit up like ___ a Christ - mas tree. ___

101

The Little Boy That Santa Claus Forgot

Words and Music by Michael Carr, Tommy Connor and Jimmy Leach

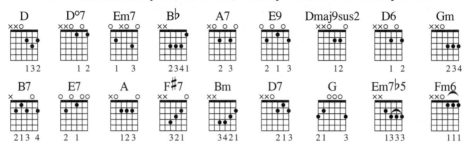

Strum Pattern: 4
Pick Pattern: 3

Intro
Slowly

Verse

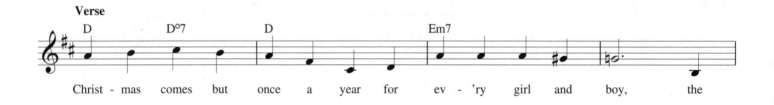

Christ - mas comes but once a year for ev - 'ry girl and boy, the

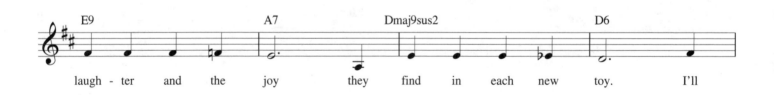

laugh - ter and the joy they find in each new toy. I'll

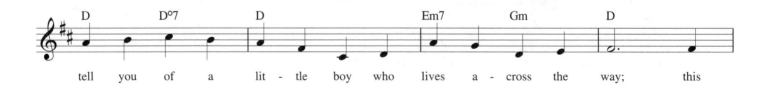

tell you of a lit - tle boy who lives a - cross the way; this

lit - tle fel - ler's Christ - mas is just an - oth - er day. He's the

Copyright © 1937 Shapiro, Bernstein & Co., New York
Copyright Renewed
International Copyright Secured   All Rights Reserved
Used by Permission

Little Saint Nick

Words and Music by Brian Wilson and Mike Love

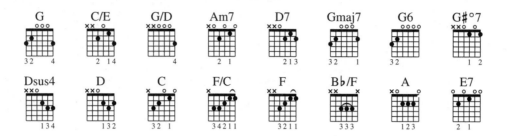

Strum Pattern: 1, 3
Pick Pattern: 4, 5

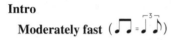

Ooh, mer - ry Christ - mas Saint Nick. _____ Ooh. _____ 1. Well, ___
(Christ - mas comes this time each year.) _

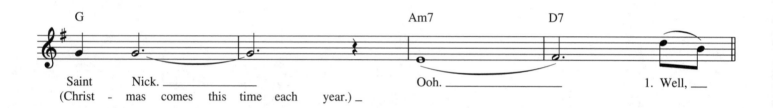

way up north where the air gets cold, ___ there's a tale a - bout Christ - mas that you've
2., 3. *See additional lyrics*

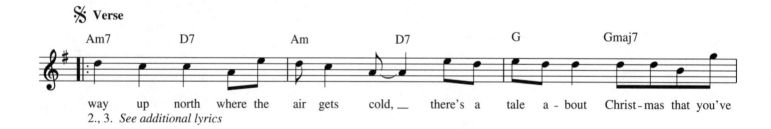

all been told. ___ And a real fa - mous cat all dressed up in red, ___ and he

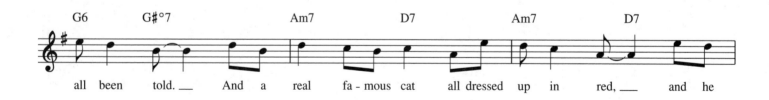

spends the whole _ year work - in' out on his sled. ___ It's the Lit - tle Saint Nick. (Lit - tle

Copyright © 1963 IRVING MUSIC, INC.
Copyright Renewed
All Rights Reserved   Used by Permission

To Coda ⊕

Am7 — Dsus4 — D — Dsus4 — D

1. | 2.

Saint Nick.)   It's the Lit - tle Saint Nick. (Lit - tle Saint Nick.) 2. Just a Saint Nick.)

Bridge

C   F/C   C   F   B♭/F   F

Run, run, rein - deer. _____   Run, run, rein - deer. Oh. _____

C   F/C   C   A   N.C.

Run, run, rein - deer. _____   Run, run, rein - deer. He don't miss no one. 3. And

⊕ **Coda**

Outro

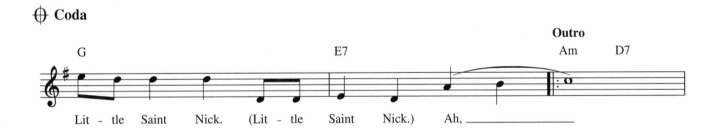

G   E7   Am   D7

Lit - tle Saint Nick. (Lit - tle Saint Nick.) Ah, _____

Repeat and fade

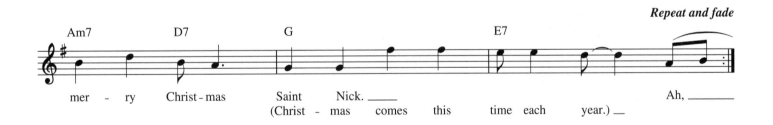

Am7   D7   G   E7

mer - ry Christ - mas Saint Nick. _____
(Christ - mas comes this time each year.) _   Ah, _____

Additional Lyrics

2. Just a little bobsled, we call it Old Saint Nick,
But she'll walk a toboggan with a four-speed stick.
She's candy-apple red with a ski for a wheel,
And when Santa hits the gas, man, just watch her peel.

3. And haulin' through the snow at a fright'nin' speed
With a half a dozen deer with Rudy to lead.
He's gotta wear his goggles 'cause the snow really flies,
And he's cruisin' ev'ry pad with a little surprise.

Merry Christmas, Darling

Words and Music by Richard Carpenter and Frank Pooler

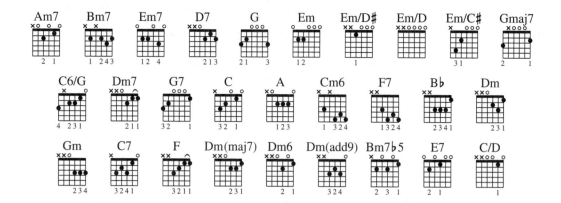

Strum Pattern: 4
Pick Pattern: 4

Intro

Freely

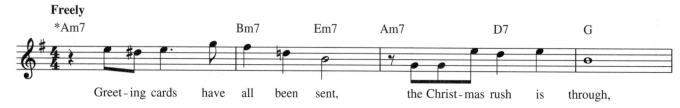

Greet-ing cards have all been sent, the Christ-mas rush is through,

*Let chords ring throughout Intro

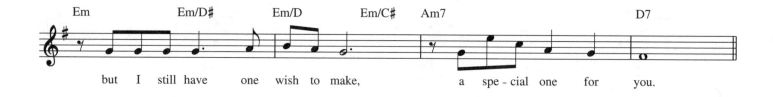

but I still have one wish to make, a spe-cial one for you.

Verse
Moderately slow

Mer-ry Christ-mas, dar-ling, We're a-part, that's true; but

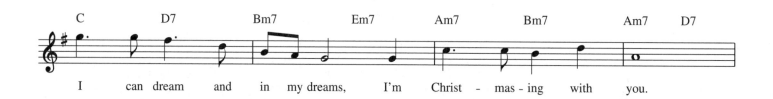

I can dream and in my dreams, I'm Christ-mas-ing with you.

Copyright © 1970 IRVING MUSIC, INC.
Copyright Renewed
All Rights Reserved   Used by Permission

Gmaj7   C6/G   Gmaj7   Dm7   G7

Hol - i - days are joy - ful, there's al - ways some - thing new. But

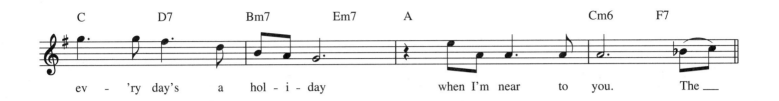

C   D7   Bm7   Em7   A   Cm6   F7

ev - 'ry day's a hol - i - day when I'm near to you. The __

𝄉 Bridge

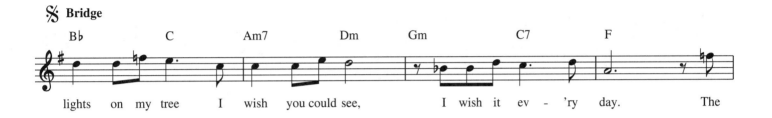

B♭   C   Am7   Dm   Gm   C7   F

lights on my tree I wish you could see, I wish it ev - 'ry day. The

Dm   Dm(maj7)   Dm7   Dm6   G   Am7   Bm7   Am7   D7

logs on the fire fill me with de - sire to see you and to __ say that I

Outro-Verse

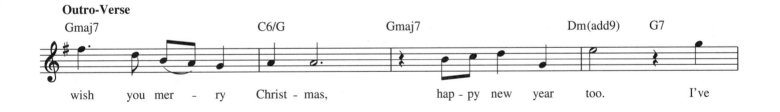

Gmaj7   C6/G   Gmaj7   Dm(add9)   G7

wish you mer - ry Christ - mas, hap - py new year too. I've

To Coda 𝄌   *D.S. al Coda*

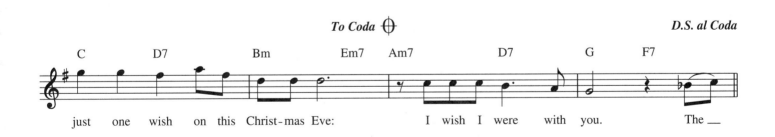

C   D7   Bm   Em7   Am7   D7   G   F7

just one wish on this Christ - mas Eve: I wish I were with you. The __

𝄌 **Coda**

Am7   D7   Bm7♭5   E7   Am7   D7   G   C/D Gmaj7

I wish I were with you. I wish I were with you. __

Merry Christmas From the Family

Words and Music by Robert Earl Keen

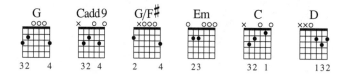

Strum Pattern: 3
Pick Pattern: 3

Mom got drunk__ and Dad got drunk__ at our Christ - mas par - ty. We were drink - in' cham - pagne punch and home - made__ egg - nog. Lit - tle sis - ter brought her new boy - friend.__ He was__ a Mex - i - can.__ We did-n't know what to think of him__ till he sang, "Fe - liz Na - vi - dad,_____ Fe - liz Na - vi - dad."_____

2. Broth - er Ken brought his kids with him,__ the three from his first wife Lynn,
3. Fran and Ri - ta drove from Har - lin - gen.__ I can't re - mem - ber how I'm kin to them.

and the two i - den - ti - cal twins__ from his sec - ond wife Mar - y Nell.____
But when they tried to plug their mo - tor home in,__ they__ blew our__ Christ - mas lights.__

© 1994 BUG MUSIC and KEEN EDGE MUSIC/ Administered by BUG MUSIC
All Rights Reserved   Used by Permission

'Course he brought his new wife Kaye,   who talks all a - bout A. A.,
Cous-in Da - vid knew just what went wrong,   so we all wait-ed out on our front lawn.

chain smok-in' while the ster-e-o plays,___   "No - el,___ No - el, the first No -
He threw the break - er and the lights came on___ and we sang, "Si - lent night, oh, si - lent

Chorus

el."_____   Carve the tur - key, turn the
night."_____   Carve the tur - key, turn the

ball game on,____ mix mar - ga - ri - tas when the egg-nog's gone.__   Send some - bod - y to the
ball game on,____ make blood - y mar - y's 'cause we all want one.__   Send some - bod - y to the

Quik - Pak store.____ We need some ice and an ex - ten - sion chord,___
Stop 'n' Go.____ We need some cel - 'ry and a can of fake snow,

a can of bean dip and some Di - et Rites,____ a box of tam - pons__ and some
a bag of lem - ons and some Di - et Sprites,____ a box of tam - pons__ and some

Marl - bo - ro Lights. ⎫ Hal - le - lu - jah, ev - 'ry - bod - y say "cheese." Mer - ry Christ - mas__ from the
Sa - lem__ Lights. ⎭

1.
fam - i - ly._____

2.
fam - i - ly._____ Fe - liz Na - vi - dad.

109

Merry Christmas Waltz

Words and Music by Bob Batson and Inex Loewer

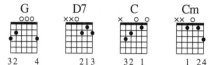

Strum Pattern: 8, 9
Pick Pattern: 7, 8

Intro
Moderate waltz

Verse

1. While we're (2.)waltz - in', while we're

{ dream - ing, } ev - 'ry - one's { dream - ing } too. Mer - ry Christ - mas, mer - ry Christ - mas, mer - ry
{ sing - ing, } { sing - ing }

Christ - mas to you. Bells are ring - in' _____ clear - er and clear - er, _____

bring - ing Christ - mas near - er and near - er. Mu - sic play - ing, cou - ples sway - ing, what a

beau - ti - ful sight, and the sea - son is the rea - son we're so hap - py to -

night. So stay in my arms, dar - ing, keep sing - in' ___ too. Mer - ry

1.
Christ - mas, mer - ry Christ - mas to you. 2. While we're

2.
you. _____

© 1955 (Renewed) Golden West Melodies, Inc.
All Rights Reserved   Used by Permission

Miracles

By Kenny G and Walter Afanasieff

Strum Pattern: 2
Pick Pattern: 4

© 1994, 2003 EMI BLACKWOOD MUSIC INC., KUZU MUSIC, KENNY G MUSIC, HIGH TECH MUSIC, SONY/ATV TUNES LLC and WALLYWORLD MUSIC
All Rights for KUZU MUSIC Controlled and Administered by EMI BLACKWOOD MUSIC INC.
All Rights for KENNY G MUSIC Administered by CAREERS-BMG MUSIC PUBLISHING, INC.
All Rights for SONY/ATV TUNES LLC and WALLYWORLD MUSIC Administered by SONY/ATV MUSIC PUBLISHING,
8 Music Square West, Nashville, TN 37203
All Rights Reserved   International Copyright Secured   Used by Permission

Merry, Merry Christmas, Baby

Words and Music by Margo Sylvia and Gilbert Lopez

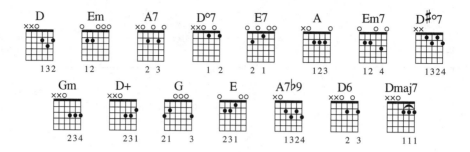

Strum Pattern: 7, 8
Pick Pattern: 7, 8

1. Mer - ry, mer - ry Christ - mas ba - by. _____

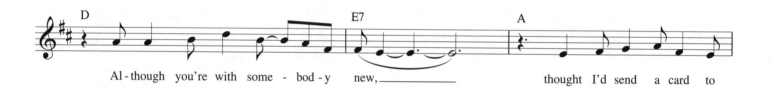

Al - though you're with some - bod - y new, _____ thought I'd send a card to

say that I wish this _ hol - i - day would find me _____ be - side _ you. _____

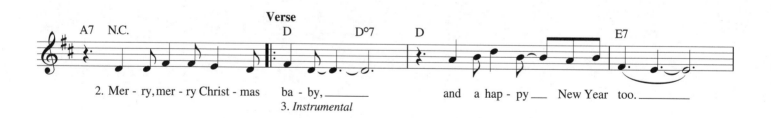

2. Mer - ry, mer - ry Christ - mas ba - by, _____ and a hap - py _ New Year too. _____
3. *Instrumental*

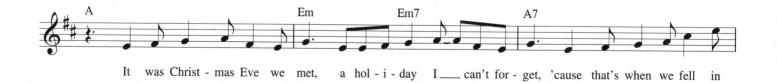

It was Christ - mas Eve we met, a hol - i - day I _ can't for - get, 'cause that's when we fell in

Copyright © 1988 by Arc Music Corporation (BMI)
International Copyright Secured All Rights Reserved
Used by Permission

love. _____   I still ____ re-mem-ber _____   the gifts we gave ___ to each

Instrumental ends

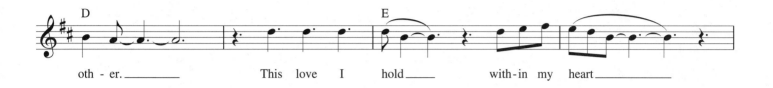

oth - er. _____   This love I hold ____ with-in my heart _____

still grows though we're ____ a - part.   Have a mer - ry, Christ - mas ba - by, _____

and a hap - py ___ New Year too. _____   I am hop - ing that you'll

find a ___ love as ___ true as mine.   Mer - ry, mer - ry Christ - mas ba - by. _____

find a ___ love as true as mine. Mer - ry, mer - ry Christ - mas ba - by. _____

*hold chord

Miss You Most at Christmas Time

Words and Music by Mariah Carey and Walter Afanasieff

Copyright © 1994 Sony/ATV Songs LLC, Rye Songs, Sony/ATV Tunes LLC and Wallyworld Music
All Rights Administered by Sony/ATV Music Publishing, 8 Music Square West, Nashville, TN 37203
International Copyright Secured   All Rights Reserved

most at Christ-mas time.___ Ooh,_____ yeah.___ 2. I

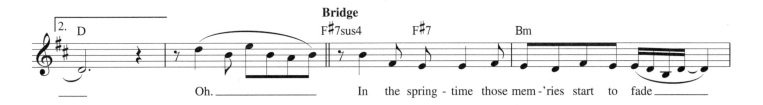

___ Oh._____ In the spring-time those mem-'ries start to fade_____

with the A - pril rain._____ Through the sum-mer days,__ till

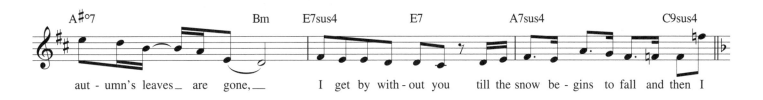

aut - umn's leaves_ are gone,__ I get by with-out you till the snow be-gins to fall and then I

Outro-Chorus

miss you_____ most at__ Christ-mas time____ and I can't get__ you, no, no, no,__

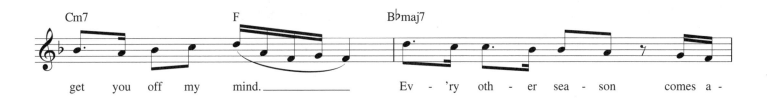

get you off my mind._____ Ev - 'ry oth - er sea - son comes a -

long and I'm al - right._____ But then I miss you most at Christ-mas__

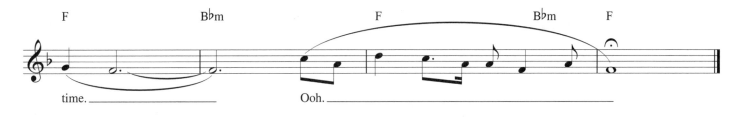

time._____ Ooh._____

Mister Santa

Words and Music by Pat Ballard

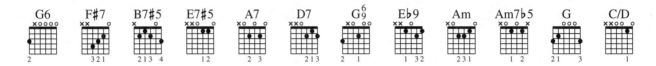

Strum Pattern: 4
Pick Pattern: 3

Brightly

Verse

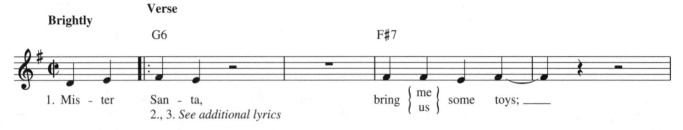

G6   F#7

1. Mis - ter San - ta, bring { me / us } some toys; ___

2., 3. *See additional lyrics*

B7#5   E7#5

bring Mer - ry Christ - mas to all girls and boys, ___

A7   D7

and ev - 'ry night { I'll / we'll } go to sleep sing - ing

G^6_9 Eb9   D7

and dream a - bout the pres - ents you'll be bring - ing.

G6   F#7   B7#5

San - ta, prom - ise { me / us } please, ___ give ev - 'ry

E7#5   Am

rein - deer a hug and a squeeze. ___ { I'll / We'll } be good, ___

© 1954, 1955 (Renewed) EDWIN H. MORRIS & COMPANY, A Division of MPL Communications, Inc.
All Rights Reserved

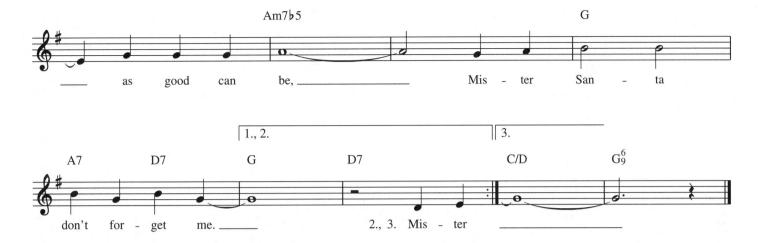

Additional Lyrics

2. Mister Santa, dear old Saint Nick
   Be awful careful and please don't get sick.
   Put on your coat when breezes are blowin'
   And when you cross the street look where you're goin'.
   Santa, we (I) love you so,
   We (I) hope you never get lost in the snow.
   Take your time when you unpack,
   Mister Santa don't hurry back.

3. Mister Santa, we've been so good.
   We've washed the dishes and done what we should.
   Made up the beds and scrubbed up our toesies.
   We've used a kleenex when we've blown our nosesies.
   Santa look at our ears, they're clean as whistles.
   We're sharper than shears.
   Now we've put you on the spot,
   Mister Santa bring us a lot.

The Night Before Christmas Song

Music by Johnny Marks
Lyrics adapted by Johnny Marks from Clement Moore's Poem

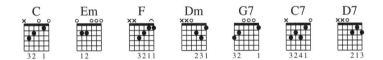

Strum Pattern: 8
Pick Pattern: 8

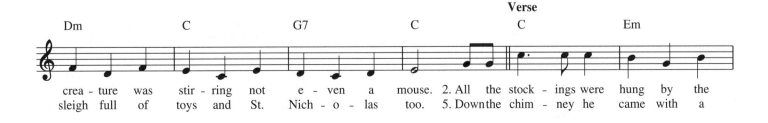

Copyright © 1952 (Renewed 1980) St. Nicholas Music Inc., 1619 Broadway, New York, New York 10019
All Rights Reserved

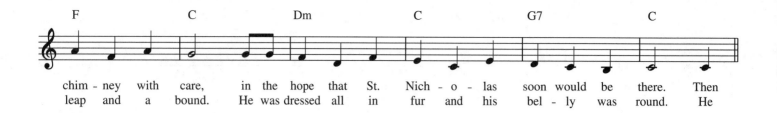

chim - ney with care, in the hope that St. Nich - o - las soon would be there. Then
leap and a bound. He was dressed all in fur and his bel - ly was round. He

Bridge

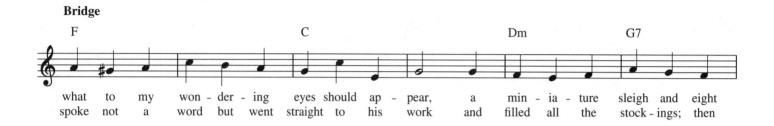

what to my won - der - ing eyes should ap - pear, a min - ia - ture sleigh and eight
spoke not a word but went straight to his work and filled all the stock - ings; then

ti - ny rein - deer. A lit - tle old driv - er so live - ly and
turned with a jerk. And lay - ing his fin - ger a - side of his

quick, I knew in a mo - ment it must be St. Nick. 3. And more
nose, then giv - ing a nod up the chim - ney he rose; 6. But I

Verse

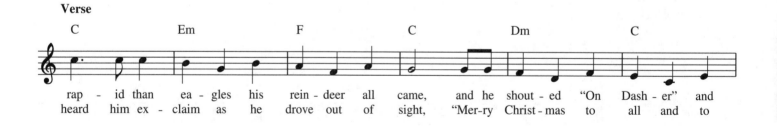

rap - id than ea - gles his rein - deer all came, and he shout - ed "On Dash - er" and
heard him ex - claim as he drove out of sight, "Mer-ry Christ - mas to all and to

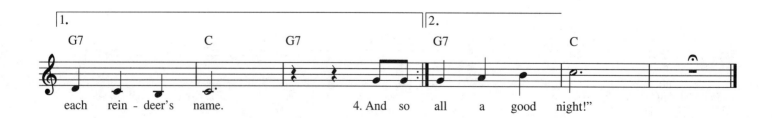

each rein - deer's name. 4. And so all a good night!"

My Favorite Things

from THE SOUND OF MUSIC
Lyrics by Oscar Hammerstein II
Music by Richard Rodgers

Strum Pattern: 7
Pick Pattern: 8

Verse
Moderately

1. Rain - drops on ros - es and whisk - ers on kit - tens, bright cop - per
2. *See additional lyrics*

ket - tles and warm wool - en mit - tens, brown pa - per pack - ag - es

tied up with strings, these are a few of my fa - vor - ite things.

fa - vor - ite things.

Outro

When the dog bites, when the

bee stings, when I'm feel - ing sad, I

sim - ply re - mem - ber my fa - vor - ite things and then I don't

feel so bad.

Additional Lyrics

2. Cream colored ponies and crisp apple strudels,
   Doorbells and sleighbells and schnitzel with noodles,
   Wild geese that fly with the moon on their wings,
   These are a few of my favorite things.

Copyright © 1959 by Richard Rodgers and Oscar Hammerstein II
Copyright Renewed
WILLIAMSON MUSIC owner of publication and allied rights throughout the world
International Copyright Secured   All Rights Reserved

The Most Wonderful Day of the Year

Music and Lyrics by Johnny Marks

Copyright © 1964 (Renewed 1992) St. Nicholas Music Inc., 1619 Broadway, New York, New York 10019
All Rights Reserved

Additional Lyrics

Intro Up at the North Pole they have their laws,
Elves must work ev'ry day.
Making the toys that Old Santa Claus
Leads upon his sleigh.

Chorus When Christmas Day is here,
The most wonderful day of the year!
Spirits gay; ev'ryone will say, "Happy Holiday!
And the best to you all the whole year through."
An electric train hidden high on a shelf
That Daddy gives David but then runs himself.
When Christmas Day is here,
The most wonderful, wonderful, wonderful,
Wonderful, wonderful day of the year!

The Most Wonderful Time of the Year

Words and Music by Eddie Pola and George Wyle

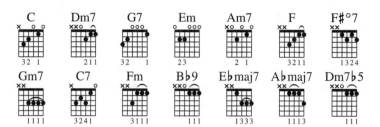

Strum Pattern: 7
Pick Pattern: 8

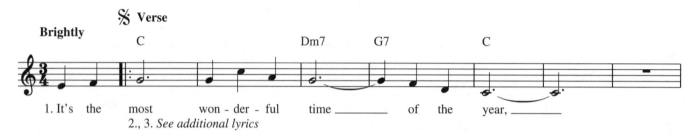

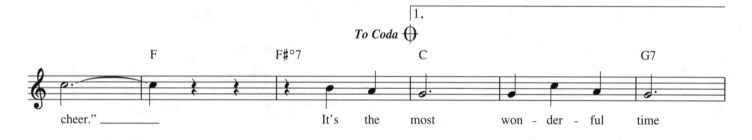

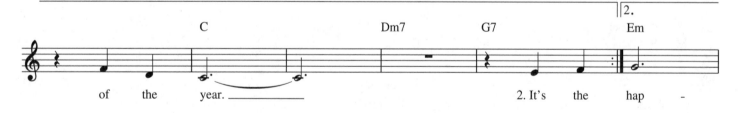

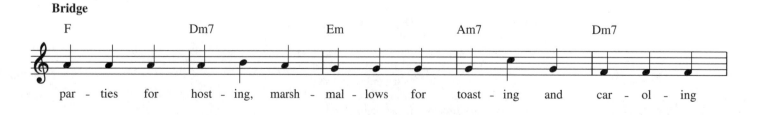

Copyright © 1963 Barnaby Music Corp.
Copyright Renewed 1991
International Copyright Secured   All Rights Reserved

out in the snow. There'll be scar - y ghost sto - ries and

D.S. al Coda

tales of the glo - ries of Christ - mas - es long, long a - go. _____ 3. It's the

⊕ Coda

most won - der - ful time, it's the most won - der - ful

time. It's the most won - der - ful time _____

_____ of the year! _____

Additional Lyrics

2. It's the hap-happiest season of all,
   With those holiday greetings
   And gay happy meetings
   When friends come to call.
   It's the hap-happiest season of all.

3. It's the most wonderful time of the year.
   There'll be much mistletoeing
   And hearts will be glowing
   When loved ones are near.
   It's the most wonderful time of the year.

Nuttin' for Christmas

Words and Music by Roy Bennett and Sid Tepper

Strum Pattern: 4
Pick Pattern: 5

Verse
Brightly

1. I broke my bat on John-ny's head; some-bod-y snitched on me. I hid a frog in
2., 3. *See additional lyrics*

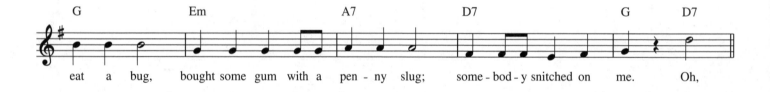

sis-ter's bed; some-bod-y snitched on me. I spilled some ink on Mom-my's rug, I made Tom-my

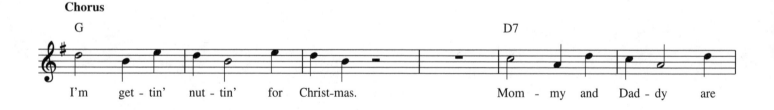

eat a bug, bought some gum with a pen-ny slug; some-bod-y snitched on me. Oh,

Chorus

I'm get-tin' nut-tin' for Christ-mas. Mom-my and Dad-dy are

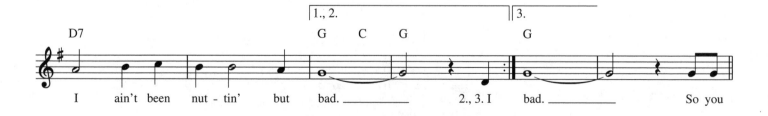

mad. I'm get-tin' nut-tin' for Christ-mas, 'cause

I ain't been nut-tin' but bad. _____ 2., 3. I bad. _____ So you

Copyright © 1955 by Chappell & Co.
Copyright Renewed
International Copyright Secured All Rights Reserved

| Am | D | G | E7 | Am7 | D7 | Bm | E7 |

bet - ter be good, what ev - er you do, 'cause if you're bad I'm warn - ing you,

| Am | D7 | G | C | G |

you'll get nut - tin' for Christ - mas. ____

Additional Lyrics

2. I put a tack on teacher's chair;
   Somebody snitched on me.
   I tied a knot in Susie's hair;
   Somebody snitched on me.
   I did a dance on Mommy's plants,
   Climbed a tree and tore my pants.
   Filled the sugar bowl with ants;
   Somebody snitched on me.

3. I won't be seeing Santa Claus;
   Somebody snitched on me.
   He won't come visit me because
   Somebody snitched on me.
   Next year, I'll be going straight.
   Next year, I'll be good, just wait.
   I'd start now but it's too late;
   Somebody snitched on me, oh,

Old Toy Trains

Words and Music by Roger Miller

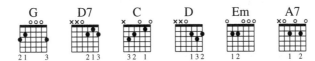

| G | D7 | C | D | Em | A7 |

Strum Pattern: 3
Pick Pattern: 3

Chorus

Moderately

Old toy trains, ___ lit - tle toy ___ tracks, ___ lit - tle toy ___ drums, ___

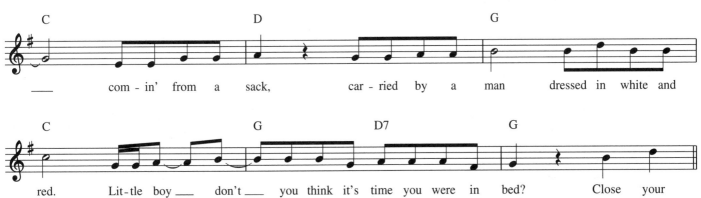

___ com - in' from a sack, car - ried by a man dressed in white and

red. Lit - tle boy ___ don't ___ you think it's time you were in bed? Close your

Copyright © 1967 Sony/ATV Songs LLC
Copyright Renewed
All Rights Administered by Sony/ATV Music Publishing, 8 Music Square West, Nashville, TN 37203
International Copyright Secured   All Rights Reserved

Bridge

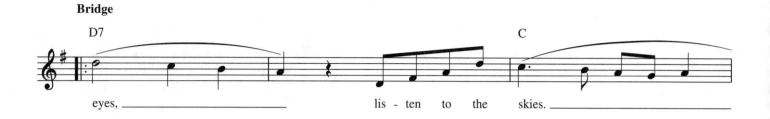

eyes, _____ lis - ten to the skies. _____

_____ All is calm, all is well; soon you'll hear Kris

Chorus

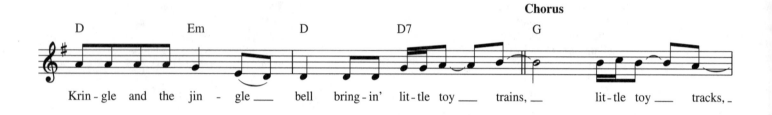

Krin - gle and the jin - gle ___ bell bring - in' lit - tle toy ___ trains, ___ lit - tle toy ___ tracks, _

___ lit - tle toy ___ drums ___ com - in' from a sack, car - ried by a

man dressed in white and red. Lit - tle boy ___ don't ___ you think it's time you were in

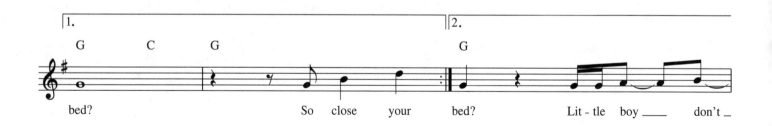

bed? So close your bed? Lit - tle boy ___ don't _

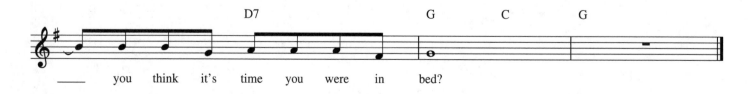

___ you think it's time you were in bed?

One Bright Star

Words and Music by John Jarvis

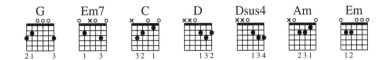

Strum Pattern: 4
Pick Pattern: 3

Intro

Moderately slow

Long, long, a-go in a world dark and cold, a night so

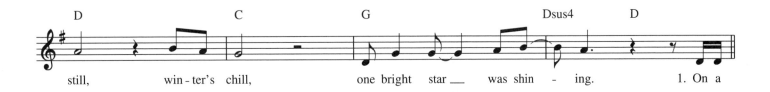

still, win-ter's chill, one bright star was shin-ing. 1. On a

Verse

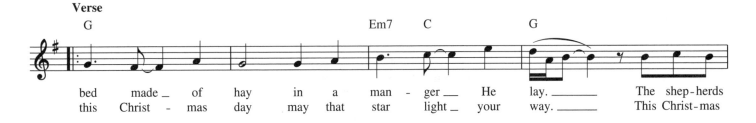

bed made of hay in a man-ger He lay. The shep-herds
this Christ-mas day may that star light your way. This Christ-mas
came, they knew His name: King of Kings, a brand new day.
Eve I still be-lieve that same star still shines on me.

Chorus

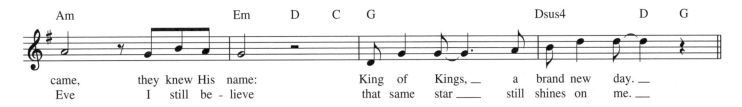

They} saw the light in the dark-ness. It shines on love and
I

ten-der-ness, brings out the hope that's in all of us. May it

Copyright © 1985 Sony/ATV Songs LLC
All Rights Administered by Sony/ATV Music Publishing, 8 Music Square West, Nashville, TN 37203
International Copyright Secured   All Rights Reserved

Am   D   G

shine   its light   on   you this Christ-mas   night.

Em7 C   Dsus4   D   G   Am

2. On   night.   May it shine   its light   on

Outro

D   G   Em7   C   G

you this Christ-mas   night.

D   C   D   G

Pretty Paper

Words and Music by Willie Nelson

Strum Pattern: 8, 7
Pick Pattern: 8, 9

Verse
Slowly, with expression

G   D7   G

1. Crowd-ed   streets,   bus-y   feet   hus-tle   by   him. _____   Down-town

D7   G   G7

shop-pers,   Christ-mas   is   nigh. _____   There he   sits   all a-lone   on the

Copyright © 1962 Sony/ATV Songs LLC
Copyright Renewed
All Rights Administered by Sony/ATV Music Publishing, 8 Music Square West, Nashville, TN 37203
International Copyright Secured All Rights Reserved

side - walk. _____ Hop - ing that you won't pass him by. _____ 2. Should you

Verse

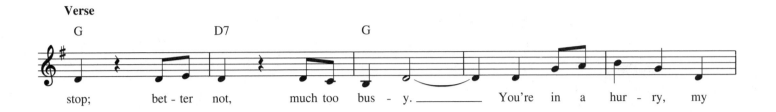

stop; bet - ter not, much too bus - y. _____ You're in a hur - ry, my

how time does fly. _____ In the dis - tance the ring - ing of ___ laugh - ter _____

___ and in the midst of the laugh - ter he cries. _____ Pret - ty

Chorus

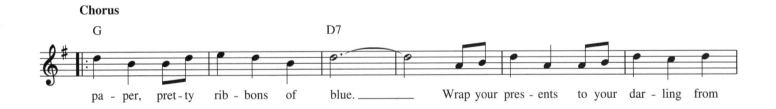

pa - per, pret - ty rib - bons of blue. _____ Wrap your pres - ents to your dar - ling from

you. _____ Pret - ty pen - cils to write, "I love you." _____ Pret - ty

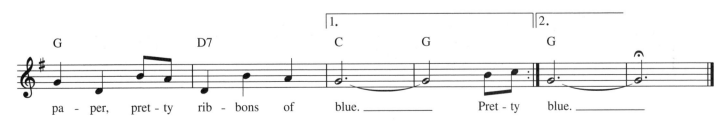

pa - per, pret - ty rib - bons of blue. _____ Pret - ty blue. _____

Please Come Home for Christmas

Words and Music by Charles Brown and Gene Redd

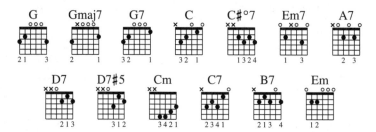

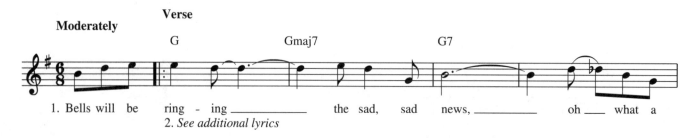

Strum Pattern: 8
Pick Pattern: 8

Moderately

Verse

1. Bells will be ring - ing _____ the sad, sad news, _____ oh ___ what a
2. *See additional lyrics*

Christ - mas _____ to have the blues! _____ My ba - by's

gone, _____ I have no friends _____ to wish me

1.

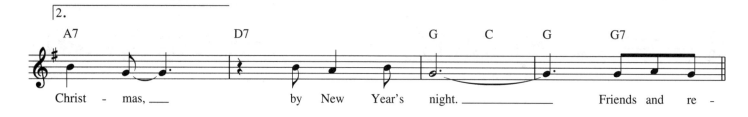

greet - ings _____ once ___ a - gain. _____ 2. Choirs will be

2.

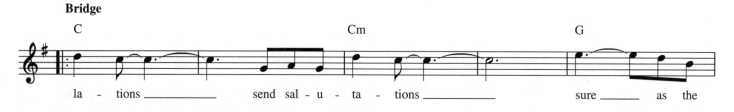

Christ - mas, ___ by New Year's night. _____ Friends and re -

Bridge

la - tions _____ send sal - u - ta - tions _____ sure _____ as the

Copyright © 1960 by Fort Knox Music Inc. and Trio Music Company, Inc.
Copyright Renewed
International Copyright Secured   All Rights Reserved
Used by Permission

stars shine a - bove. _____ For this is Christ - mas, _____ yes, Christ - mas my

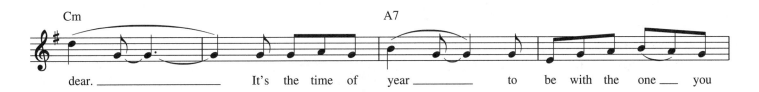

dear. _____ It's the time of year _____ to be with the one ___ you

Verse

love. 3., 4. So won't you tell me _____ you'll nev - er - more

roam, _____ Christ - mas and New Year _____ will find you at

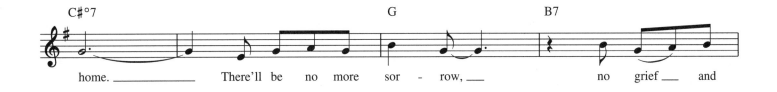

home. _____ There'll be no more sor - row, ___ no grief ___ and

pain _____ and I'll be hap - py, hap - py once _____ a -

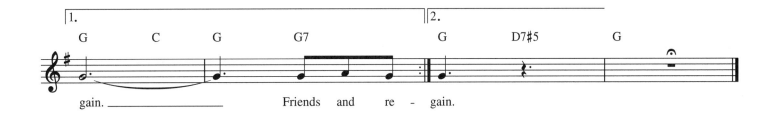

gain. _____ Friends and re - gain.

Additional Lyrics

2. Choirs will be singing "Silent Night,"
Christmas carols by candlelight.
Please come home for Christmas,
Please come home for Christmas;
If not for Christmas, by New Year's night.

Rockin' Around the Christmas Tree

Music and Lyrics by Johnny Marks

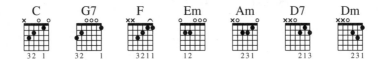

Strum Pattern: 2, 6
Pick Pattern: 4, 6

Verse
Moderate Rock

1., 2. Rock-in' a - round the Christ-mas tree __ at the Christ-mas par-ty hop. __

Mis-tle-toe hung where you can see __ ev-'ry cou-ple tries to stop.

Rock-in' a - round the Christ-mas tree, __ let the Christ-mas spir - it ring. __

Lat - er we'll have some pump-kin pie __ and we'll do some car - ol - ing.

Bridge

You will get a sen - ti - men - tal feel - ing when you hear

voic - es sing - ing, "Let's be jol - ly. Deck the halls with boughs of hol - ly."

Copyright © 1958 (Renewed 1986) St. Nicholas Music Inc., 1619 Broadway, New York, New York 10019
All Rights Reserved

Outro

Rock-in' a - round the Christ-mas tree, _ have a hap-py hol-i-day. _ Ev-'ry-one danc-ing

mer - ri - ly in the new old fash-ioned way. new old fash - ioned way. _____

Santa, Bring My Baby Back (To Me)

Words and Music by Claude DeMetruis and Aaron Schroeder

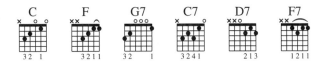

Strum Pattern: 4
Pick Pattern: 3

Verse

Moderate Rock

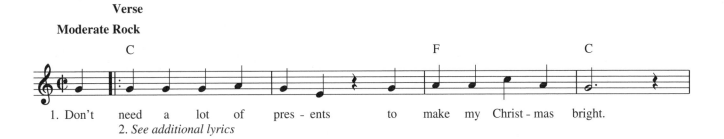

1. Don't need a lot of pres - ents to make my Christ - mas bright.
2. *See additional lyrics*

I just need my ba - by's arms wound a - round me tight. Oh, San - ta, hear my

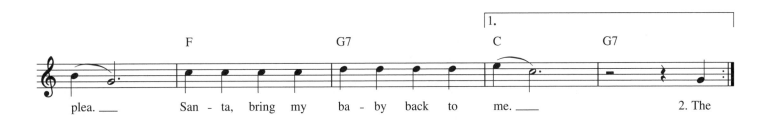

plea. _ San - ta, bring my ba - by back to me. _ 2. The

Copyright © 1957 by Gladys Music, Inc.
Copyright Renewed and Assigned to Gladys Music and Rachel's Own Music
All Rights for Gladys Music Administered by Cherry Lane Music Publishing Company, Inc. and Chrysalis Music
All Rights for Rachel's Own Music Administered by A. Schroeder International LLC
International Copyright Secured   All Rights Reserved

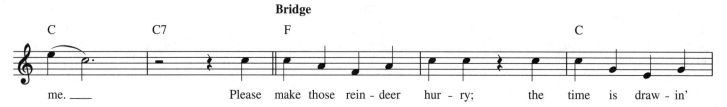

Bridge

me. ___ Please make those rein - deer hur - ry; the time is draw - in'

near. It sure won't seem like Christ - mas un - less my ba - by's here. Don't

Outro

fill my socks with can - dy, no bright and shin - y toy. You

wan - na make me hap - py and fill my heart with joy. Then, San - ta, hear my

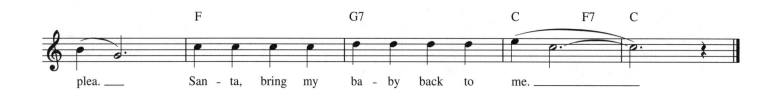

plea. ___ San - ta, bring my ba - by back to me. ___

Additional Lyrics

2. The Christmas tree is ready.
   The candles all aglow.
   But with my baby far away
   What good is mistletoe?
   Oh, Santa, hear my plea.
   Santa, bring my baby back to me.

Shake Me I Rattle
(Squeeze Me I Cry)

Words and Music by Hal Hackady and Charles Naylor

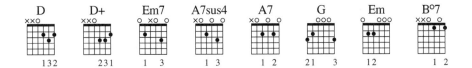

Strum Pattern: 7
Pick Pattern: 7

Intro

Moderately

Verse

I was pass - ing by a toy shop on the
called an - oth - er toy shop on a
late and snow was fall - ing as the

cor - ner of the square, where a lit - tle girl was look - ing in the win - dow
square so long a - go, where I saw a lit - tle dol - ly that I want - ed
shop - pers hur - ried by past the girl - ie at the win - dow with her lit - tle head held

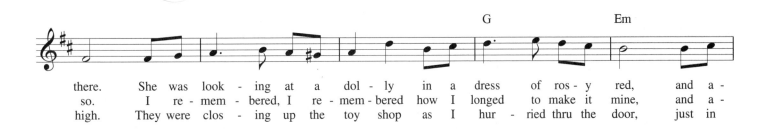

there. She was look - ing at a dol - ly in a dress of ros - y red, and a -
so. I re - mem - bered, I re - mem - bered how I longed to make it mine, and a -
high. They were clos - ing up the toy shop as I hur - ried thru the door, just in

Chorus

round the pret - ty dol - ly hung a lit - tle sign that said: } Shake me, I
round that oth - er dol - ly hung an - oth - er lit - tle sign: }
time to buy the dol - ly that her heart was long - ing for. }

rat - tle, squeeze me I cry. { As I stood there be - side her
{ I had count - ed my pen - nies.
And I gave her the dol - ly that we

Copyright © 1957 (Renewed) by Regent Music Corporation (BMI)
International Copyright Secured   All Rights Reserved
Used by Permission

I could hear her sigh.
Just a pen-ny shy.
both had longed to buy.

Shake me I rat-tle, squeeze me I
cry. Please take me home and love__ me.__

1. I re -
2. It was

This Christmas

Words and Music by Donny Hathaway and Nadine McKinnor

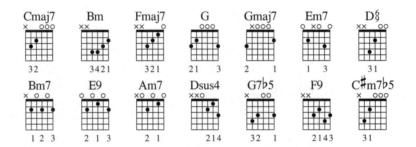

*Strum Pattern: 2
*Pick Pattern: 4

Intro

Moderately

* Use Patterns 7 & 9 for ¾ meas.

1., 4. Hang all the mis-tle-toe.__ I'm gon-na get to know you bet-ter,__
2. Pres-ents and cards are here.__ My world is filled with cheer and you,__
3. *Instrumental*

this Christ-mas. And as we trim the tree,__ how much fun it's gon-na be to-
this Christ-mas. And as I look a-round,__ your__ eyes out-shine the town; they

Copyright © 1970 by BMG Songs, Inc., Kuumba Music Publishing and Crystal Raisin Music
Copyright Renewed
All Rights for Kuumba Music Publishing Administered by BMG Songs, Inc.
International Copyright Secured   All Rights Reserved

Rudolph the Red-Nosed Reindeer

Music and Lyrics by Johnny Marks

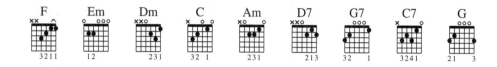

Intro
Freely

You know Dash-er and Danc-er and Pranc-er and Vix-en, Com-et and Cu-pid and

Don-ner and Blitz-en, but do you re-call the most fa-mous rein-deer of all?

Strum Pattern: 2, 3
Pick Pattern: 2, 3

Verse

Lightly

1., 2. Ru-dolph, the red-nosed rein-deer had a ver-y shin-y nose,

and if you ev-er saw it, you would e-ven say it glows.

All of the oth-er rein-deer used to laugh and call him names,

Copyright © 1949 (Renewed 1977) St. Nicholas Music Inc., 1619 Broadway, New York, New York 10019
All Rights Reserved

they nev - er let poor Ru - dolph join in an - y rein - deer games.

Bridge

Then one fog - gy Christ - mas Eve, San - ta came to say,

"Ru - dolph, with your nose so bright, won't you guide my sleigh to - night?" _

Outro

Then how the rein - deer loved him as they shout - ed out with glee;

1.

"Ru - dolph, the red - nosed rein - deer, you'll go down in his - to - ry!"

2.

you'll go down in his - to - ry!" _____

Share Love

Words and Music by Nathan Morris

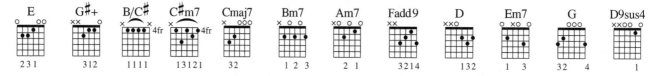

Strum Pattern: 1, 2
Pick Pattern: 2, 4

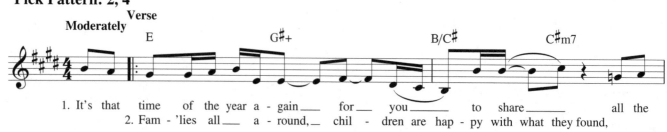

1. It's that time of the year a- gain___ for___ you___ to share___ all the
2. Fam - 'lies all___ a - round,___ chil - dren are hap - py with what they found,

love___ that you have___ with ev - 'ry wom - an and ev - 'ry man,___ to share___ love.___
giv - ing things on this day and thank - ing our God, for teach - ing us the way to share___ love.___

___ Christ - mas Day___ is here and the Lord___
___ As the snow is fall - ing down, pres - ents un - wrapped un -

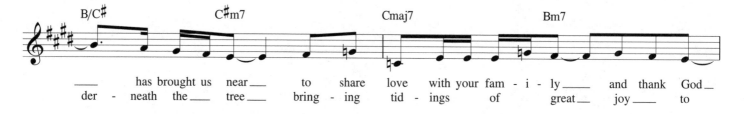

___ has brought us near___ to share love with your fam - i - ly___ and thank God___
der - neath the___ tree___ bring - ing tid - ings of great___ joy___ to

___ for al - low - ing you___ to see that
ev - 'ry lit - tle girl and___ boy. You know

Christ - mas is___ the___ time___

___ to share___ with the one you love. Share___ good___ things,___ joy,

Copyright © 1993 by Vanderpool Publishing and Ensign Music Corporation
International Copyright Secured All Rights Reserved

and glad tid - ings.___ Share love. Giv - ing all___ you___ have___ this day___ lets the world

1.

know that you care___ and you___ will be there___ to share love.___

2. **Bridge**

___ Now,_____ the true_____ mean - ing of Christ - mas____ is

fall - ing on___ your knees____ and thank - ing the Lord___ for what He's done, giv - ing the world___

___ His on - ly Son._____ Oh,_____ ooh,___ let Him

Outro-Chorus

in.

Christ - mas is___ the___ time___ to share with the one you love. Share___ good___ things,___ joy,

*Vocal overlap. Omit upstem note on repeats.

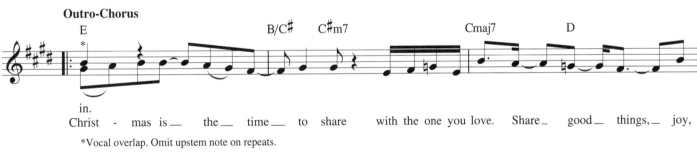

and glad tid - ings. Share___ love. Giv - ing all___ you___ have___ this day lets the world

Repeat and fade

know that you care_____ and_____ you will be there_____ to share___ love.

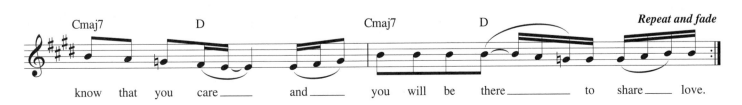

Silver and Gold

Music and Lyrics by Johnny Marks

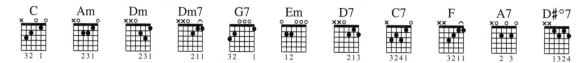

Strum Pattern: 8
Pick Pattern: 8

Verse
Slowly

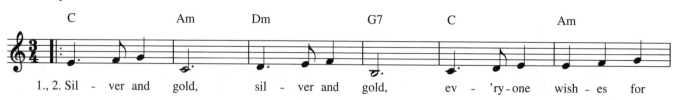

1., 2. Sil - ver and gold, sil - ver and gold, ev - 'ry-one wish - es for

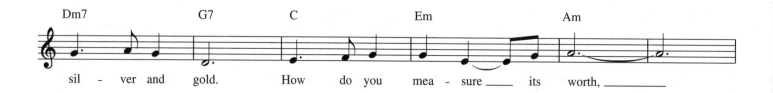

sil - ver and gold. How do you mea - sure _____ its worth, _____

just by the plea - sure _____ it gives here on earth? Sil - ver and gold,

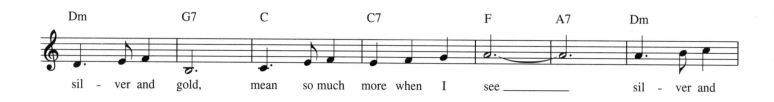

sil - ver and gold, mean so much more when I see _____ sil - ver and

gold dec - o - ra - tions _____ on ev - 'ry Christ - mas tree. _____ tree. _____

Copyright © 1964 (Renewed 1992) St. Nicholas Music Inc., 1619 Broadway, New York, New York 10019
All Rights Reserved

Silver Bells

from the Paramount Picture THE LEMON DROP KID
Words and Music by Jay Livingston and Ray Evans

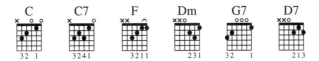

Strum Pattern: 9
Pick Pattern: 8

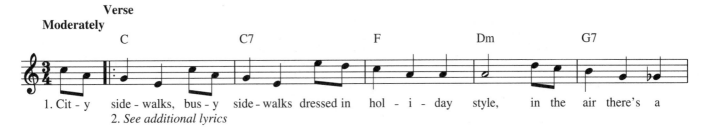

Additional Lyrics

2. Strings of street lights, even stop lights
Blink a bright red and green,
As the shoppers rush home with their treasures.
Hear the snow crunch, see the kids bunch,
This is Santa's big scene,
And above all the bustle you hear:

Copyright © 1950 (Renewed 1977) by Paramount Music Corporation
International Copyright Secured   All Rights Reserved

Some Children See Him

Lyric by Wihla Hutson
Music by Alfred Burt

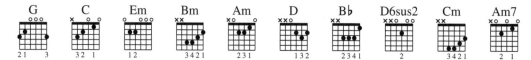

*Strum Pattern: 7 & 10
*Pick Pattern: 7 & 10

Verse

Slowly

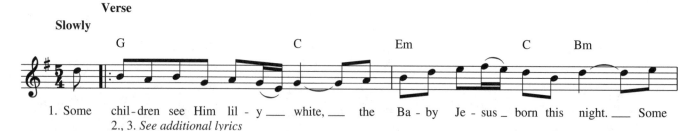

1. Some chil-dren see Him lil-y __ white, __ the Ba-by Je-sus __ born this night. __ Some
2., 3. *See additional lyrics*

*Combine Patterns for ⁵⁄₄

chil-dren see Him lil-y __ white, __ with tress-es soft and __ fair. Some

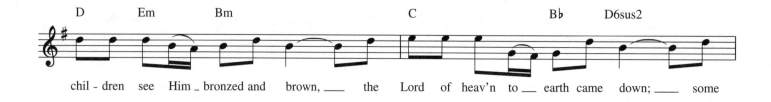

chil-dren see Him _ bronzed and brown, __ the Lord of heav'n to __ earth came down; __ some

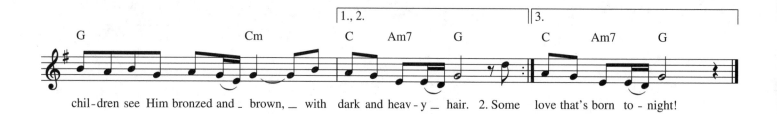

chil-dren see Him bronzed and _ brown, _ with dark and heav-y _ hair. 2. Some love that's born to-night!

Additional Lyrics

2. Some children see Him almond eyed,
   This Savior whom we kneel beside.
   Some children see Him almond eyed,
   With skin of yellow hue.
   Some children see Him dark as they,
   Sweet Mary's Son to whom we pray;
   Some children see Him dark as they,
   And ah! They love Him too!

3. The children in each diff'rent place
   Will see the Baby Jesus' face
   Like theirs, but bright with heav'nly grace;
   And filled with holy light.
   O lay aside each earthly thing,
   And with thy heart as offering,
   Come worship now the infant King,
   'Tis love that's born tonight!

TRO - © Copyright 1954 (Renewed) and 1957 (Renewed) Hollis Music, Inc., New York, NY
International Copyright Secured
All Rights Reserved Including Public Performance For Profit
Used by Permission

The Star Carol

Lyric by Wihla Hutson

Music by Alfred Burt

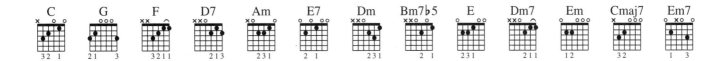

Strum Pattern: 8
Pick Pattern: 8

Verse
Tenderly

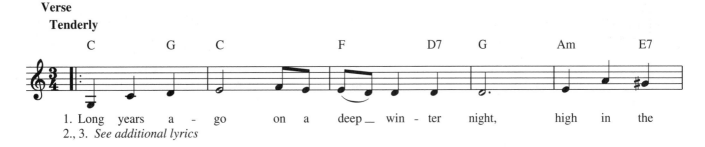

1. Long years a - go on a deep __ win - ter night, high in the
2., 3. *See additional lyrics*

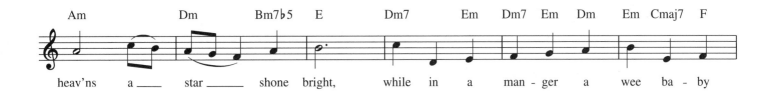

heav'ns a __ star __ shone bright, while in a man - ger a wee ba - by

lay. Sweet - ly a - sleep on a bed of hay. Thee.

Additional Lyrics

2. Jesus, the Lord was that Baby so small,
   Laid down to sleep in a humble stall;
   Then came the star and it stood overhead,
   Shedding its light 'round His little bed.

3. Dear Baby Jesus, how tiny Thou art,
   I'll make a place for Thee in my heart,
   And when the stars in the heavens I see,
   Ever and always I'll think of Thee.

TRO - © Copyright 1954 (Renewed) and 1957 (Renewed) Hollis Music, Inc., New York, NY
International Copyright Secured
All Rights Reserved Including Public Performance For Profit
Used by Permission

Someday At Christmas

Words and Music by Ronald N. Miller and Bryan Wells

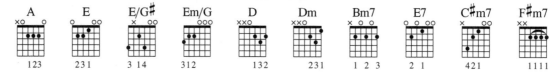

Strum Pattern: 3, 4
Pick Pattern: 3, 6

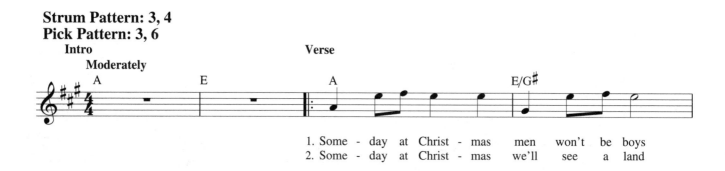

1. Some - day at Christ - mas men won't be boys
2. Some - day at Christ - mas we'll see a land

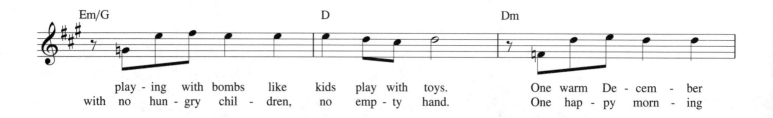

play - ing with bombs like kids play with toys. One warm De - cem - ber
with no hun - gry chil - dren, no emp - ty hand. One hap - py morn - ing

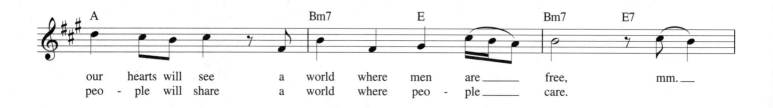

our hearts will see a world where men are free, mm.
peo - ple will share a world where peo - ple care.

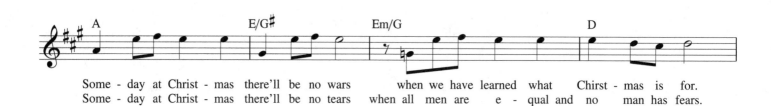

Some - day at Christ - mas there'll be no wars when we have learned what Chirst - mas is for.
Some - day at Christ - mas there'll be no tears when all men are e - qual and no man has fears.

When we have found what life's real - ly worth there'll be peace on earth.
One shin - ing mo - ment, one prayer a - way from our world to - day.

© 1966 (Renewed 1994) JOBETE MUSIC CO., INC. and STONE DIAMOND MUSIC CORP.
All Rights for JOBETE MUSIC CO., INC. Controlled and Administered by EMI APRIL MUSIC INC.
All Rights for STONE DIAMOND MUSIC CORP. Controlled and Administered by EMI BLACKWOOD MUSIC INC.
All Rights Reserved   International Copyright Secured   Used by Permission

Chorus

Some-day all our dreams will come to be, some-day in a world where men are free, —

may-be not in time for you and me, — but some-day at Christ-mas time.

Verse

3. Some-day at Christ-mas man will not fail; hate will be gone and love — will pre-vail.

Some-day a new world that we can start — with hope in ev-'ry heart. —

Outro-Chorus

Some-day all our dreams will come to be, some-day in a world where

men are free, may-be not in time for you and me, — but

some-day at Christ-mas time, some-day at Christ-mas time.

Suzy Snowflake

Words and Music by Sid Tepper and Roy Bennett

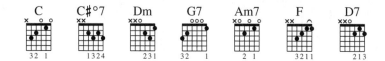

Strum Pattern: 3
Pick Pattern: 3

Copyright © 1951 by Chappell & Co.
Copyright Renewed
International Copyright Secured All Rights Reserved

This Is Christmas
(Bright, Bright the Holly Berries)

Lyric by Wihla Hutson
Music by Alfred Burt

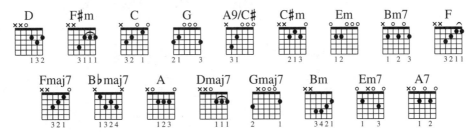

Strum Pattern: 7, 9
Pick Pattern: 7, 8

Verse
Liltingly

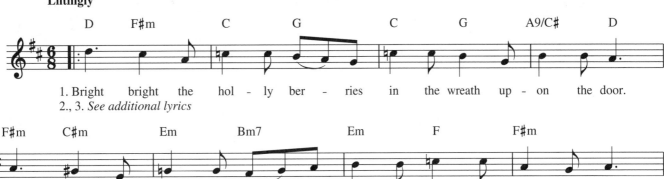

1. Bright bright the hol-ly ber-ries in the wreath up-on the door.
2., 3. *See additional lyrics*

Bright, bright the hap-py fac-es with the thoughts of joys in store.

White, white the snow-y mead-ow wrapped in slum-ber deep and sweet.

White, white the mis-tle-toe ___ 'neath which two lov-ers meet.

[1., 2.]   [3.]

Chorus

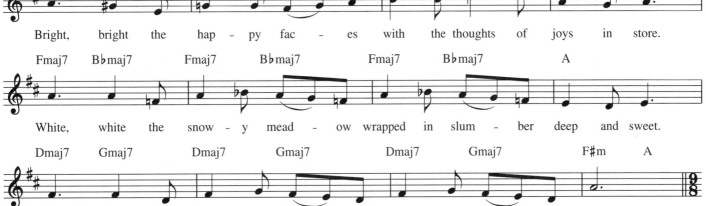

This is Christ-mas, this is Christ-mas, this is Christ-mas time. ___ ___

Additional Lyrics

2. Gay, gay the children's voices filled with laughter, filled with glee.
   Gay, gay the tinsled things upon the dark and spicy tree.
   Day, day when all mankind may hear the angel's song again.
   Day, day when Christ was born to bless the sons of men.

3. Sing, sing ye heav'nly host to tell the blessed Saviour's birth.
   Sing, sing in holy joy, ye dwellers all upon the earth.
   King, King yet tiny Babe, come down to us from God above.
   King, King of ev'ry heart which opens wide to love.

TRO - © Copyright 1954 (Renewed) and 1957 (Renewed) Hollis Music, Inc., New York, NY
International Copyright Secured
All Rights Reserved Including Public Performance For Profit
Used by Permission

This One's for the Children

Words and Music by Maurice Starr

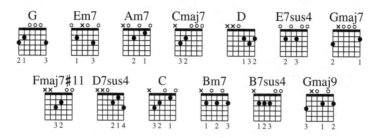

Strum Pattern: 4
Pick Pattern: 3

Verse

Slowly

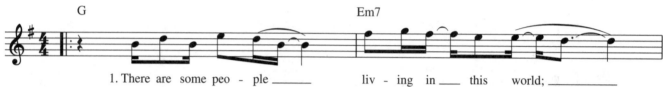

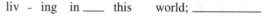

1. There are some peo - ple _____ liv - ing in ___ this world; _____
2. *See additional lyrics*

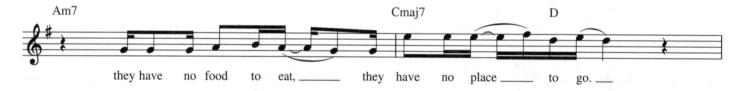

they have no food to eat, _____ they have no place _____ to go. ___

But we all are God's chil - dren, we have to learn to love _ one an - oth - er. ___

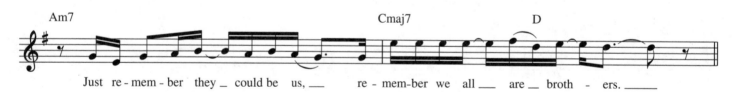

Just re - mem - ber they _ could be us, ___ re - mem - ber we all ___ are _ broth - ers. ___

Pre-Chorus

I'm not try - ing ___ to dark - en up _ your day, ___ but help oth - ers in need _ and

𝄋 Chorus

show them there's a bet - ter ___ way. _ This one's for the chil - dren, ___

© 1989 EMI APRIL MUSIC INC. and MAURICE STARR MUSIC
All Rights Controlled and Administered by EMI APRIL MUSIC INC.
All Rights Reserved   International Copyright Secured   Used by Permission

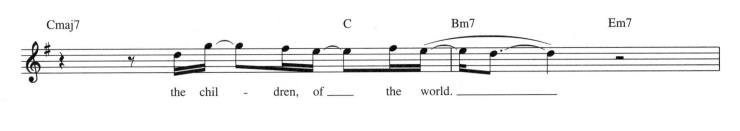

the chil - dren, of _____ the world. _____

This one's for the chil - dren. _____

To Coda ⊕

May God keep them _____ in His _____ throne. _____ Oo. _____

D.S. al Coda

_____ throne. _____ This one's for the chil -

⊕ **Coda**

_____ throne. _____ The chil - dren _ of the world. _____ This one's for the chil -

Outro

Repeat and fade

- dren. This one's for the chil - dren.

Additional Lyrics

2. Many people are happy
And many people are sad.
Some people have many things
That others can only wish they had.
So, for the sake of the children,
Show them love's the only way to go
'Cause they're our tomorrow,
And people they've got to know.

We Need a Little Christmas

from MAME

Music and Lyric by Jerry Herman

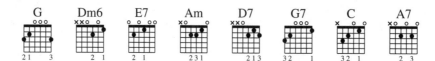

Strum Pattern: 4
Pick Pattern: 1

Verse

Brightly

G

1. Haul out the hol - ly. _____ Put up the
climb down the chim - ney, _____ turn on the

tree be - fore my spir - it falls _____ a - gain.
bright - est string of lights I've ev - er seen.

Fill up the stock - ing. _____ I may be
Slice up the fruit - cake. _____ It's time we

rush - ing things, but deck the halls _____ a - gain
hung some tin - sel on the ev - er - green

now. _____
bough. _____

For we
For I've
For we

need a lit - tle Christ - mas, right this ver - y min - ute,
grown a lit - tle lean - er, grown a lit - tle cold - er,
need a lit - tle mu - sic, need a lit - tle laugh - ter,

© 1966 (Renewed) JERRY HERMAN
All Rights Controlled by JERRYCO MUSIC CO.
Exclusive Agent: EDWIN H. MORRIS & COMPANY, A Division of MPL Communications, Inc.
All Rights Reserved

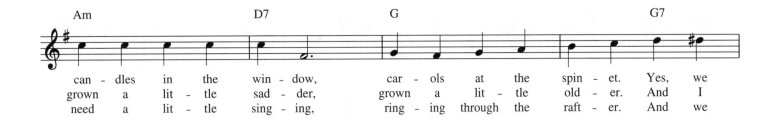

can - dles in the win - dow, car - ols at the spin - et. Yes, we
grown a lit - tle sad - der, grown a lit - tle old - er. And I
need a lit - tle sing - ing, ring - ing through the raft - er. And we

To Coda ⊕

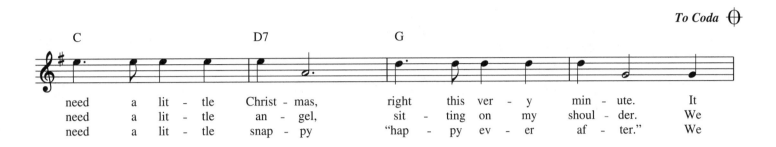

need a lit - tle Christ - mas, right this ver - y min - ute. It
need a lit - tle an - gel, sit - ting on my shoul - der. We
need a lit - tle snap - py "hap - py ev - er af - ter." We

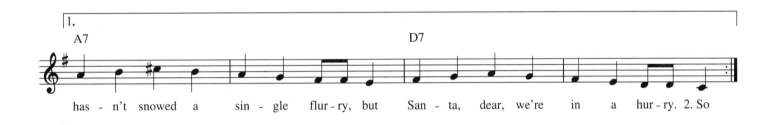

has - n't snowed a sin - gle flur - ry, but San - ta, dear, we're in a hur - ry. 2. So

D.S. al Coda

need a lit - tle Christ - mas now!

⊕ **Coda**

need a lit - tle Christ - mas now! _____

What a Merry Christmas This Could Be

Words and Music by Hank Cochran and Harlan Howard

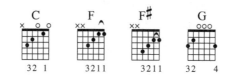

Strum Pattern: 3
Pick Pattern: 3

Chorus
Moderate Country

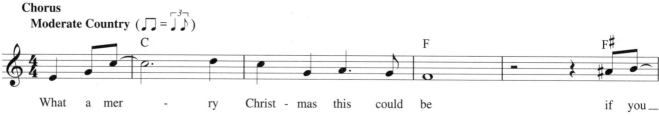

What a mer - ry Christ - mas this could be if you__

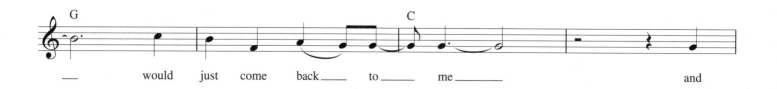

__ would just come back__ to__ me__ and

say that you'd for - giv - en__ me.__ What a mer -

- ry Christ - mas this__ could__ be.__

Verse

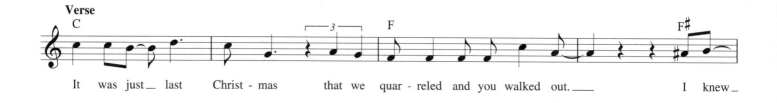

It was just__ last Christ - mas that we quar - reled and you walked out.__ I knew__

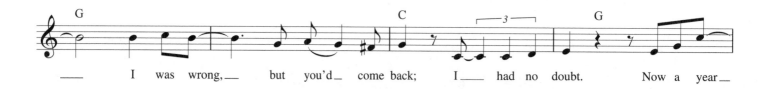

__ I was wrong,__ but you'd come back; I__ had no doubt. Now a year__

Copyright © 1964 Sony/ATV Songs LLC
Copyright Renewed
All Rights Administered by Sony/ATV Music Publishing, 8 Music Square West, Nashville, TN 37203
International Copyright Secured   All Rights Reserved

has rolled a - round, __ it's Christ-mas once a - gain, and

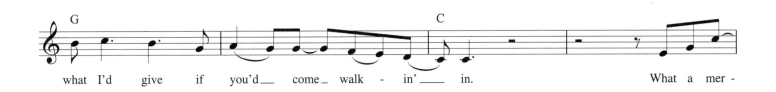

what I'd give if you'd__ come_ walk - in'__ in. What a mer -

Chorus

- ry Christ - mas this could be if you__

2nd time, Instrumental

__ would just come back__ to __ me __ and

say that you'd for - giv - en __ me. __ What a mer -

- ry Christ - mas this_ could_ be. __ *Instrumental begins* What a mer -

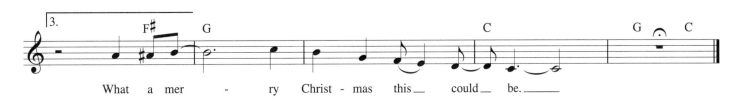

What a mer - ry Christ - mas this_ could_ be. __

155

What Are You Doing New Year's Eve?

By Frank Loesser

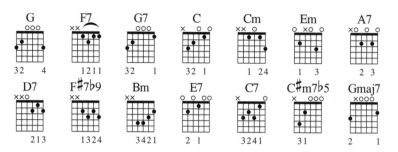

Strum Pattern: 5
Pick Pattern: 5

Verse

Moderately

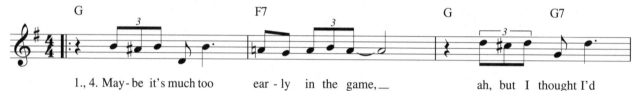

1., 4. May-be it's much too ear-ly in the game, ___ ah, but I thought I'd

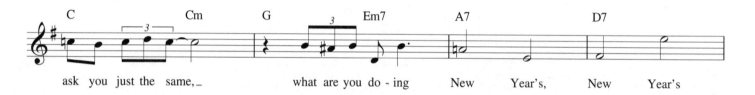

ask you just the same, ___ what are you do-ing New Year's, New Year's

Verse

Eve? 2., 5. Won-der whose arms will hold you good and tight, ___

when it's ex-act-ly twelve o'-clock that night, ___ wel-com-ing in the

Bridge

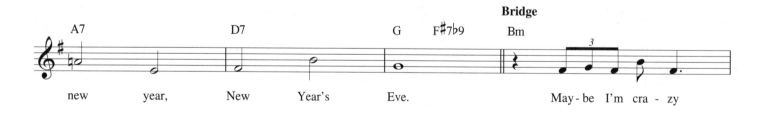

new year, New Year's Eve. May-be I'm cra-zy

to sup-pose I'd ev-er be the one you chose

© 1947 (Renewed) FRANK MUSIC CORP.
All Rights Reserved

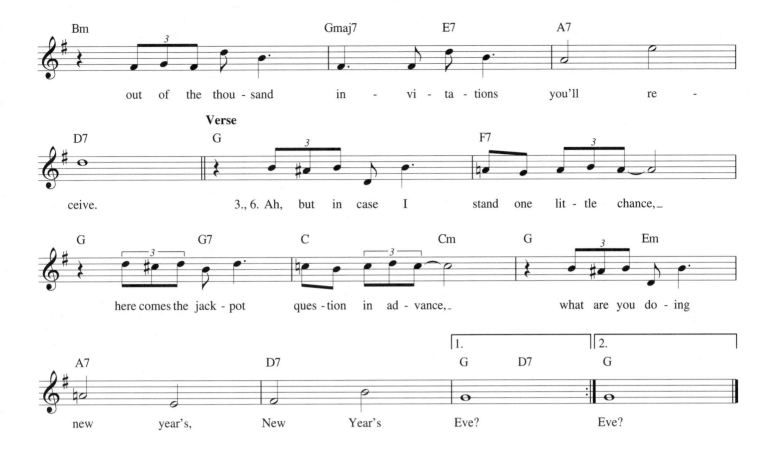

out of the thou - sand in - vi - ta - tions you'll re - ceive.

3., 6. Ah, but in case I stand one lit - tle chance,_

here comes the jack - pot ques - tion in ad - vance,_ what are you do - ing new year's, New Year's Eve? Eve?

The White World of Winter

Words by Mitchell Parish
Music by Hoagy Carmichael

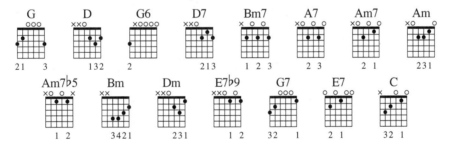

Strum Pattern: 4
Pick Pattern: 3

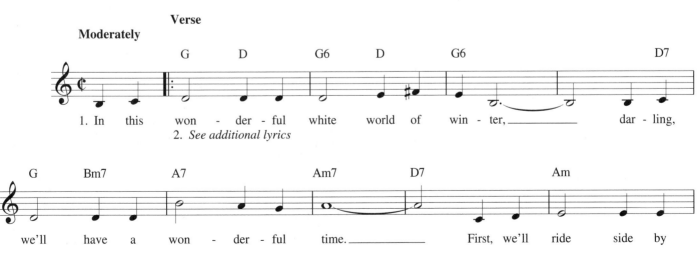

1. In this won - der - ful white world of win - ter,_____ dar - ling,
2. *See additional lyrics*

we'll have a won - der - ful time._____ First, we'll ride side by

Copyright © 1965 by Songs Of Peer, Ltd. and Cromwell Music, Inc., New York, NY
Copyright Renewed
International Copyright Secured   All Rights Reserved

Additional Lyrics

2. In this wonderful white world of winter,
Darling, we'll have a wonderful time;
If we prayed it would snow all this winter
I as ya, is that a terr'ble, horr'ble crime?
I can't wait till we skate on Lake Happy
And sup a hot buttered cup in the afterglow.
If there's ever a moment you're not laughin',
Maybe a toboggan; split your little noggin'.
In this wonderful white world of winter,
I'm thinkin' you are the sweetest one I know.

What Christmas Means to Me

Words and Music by George Gordy, Allen Story and Anna Gordy Gaye

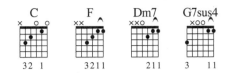

Intro
Brightly

Verse

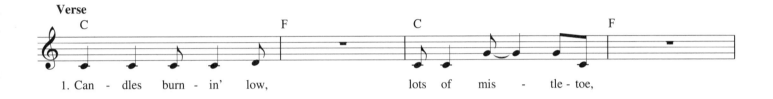

1. Can - dles burn - in' low, lots of mis - tle - toe,

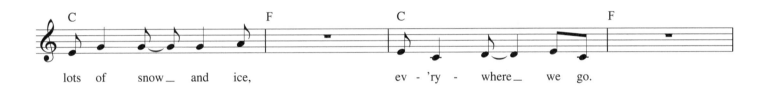

lots of snow and ice, ev - 'ry - where we go.

Choirs sing - in' car - ols right out - side my door.

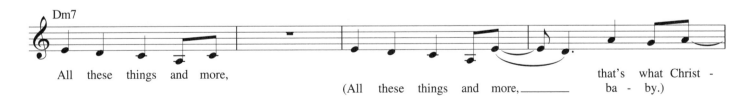

All these things and more, that's what Christ -
(All these things and more, ba - by.)

- mas means to me, my love. (That's what Christ - mas means to me, my love.)

© 1967 (Renewed 1995) JOBETE MUSIC CO., INC.
All Rights Controlled and Administered by EMI BLACKWOOD MUSIC INC. on behalf of STONE AGATE MUSIC (A Division of JOBETE MUSIC CO., INC.)
All Rights Reserved   International Copyright Secured   Used by Permission

Interlude

2. I ___

Verse

see your smil - ing face like I nev - er seen ___ be - fore. ___ E -

- ven though ___ I love ___ you mad - ly, it seems I love you more. The lit -

- tle cards ___ you'll give ___ me will touch ___ my heart ___ for sure. All ___

___ these things ___ and more, ___ dar - lin',
(All these things and more, ___ dar - lin'.)
that's what Christ -

- mas means ___ to me, ___ my love. (That's what Christ - mas means to me, ___ my love.) ___

Bridge

I feel ___ like run - nin' wild, ___ as anx - ious as a lit - tle child to greet ___

___ you 'neath ___ the mis - tle - toe, kiss you once ___ and then ___ some more. And

Dm7

wish you a mer - ry Christ - mas, ba - by, and such (Wish you a mer - ry Christ - mas, ba - by.)

G7sus4

hap - pi - ness in the com - ing year. __ Whoa, ba - by. 3. Let's deck __

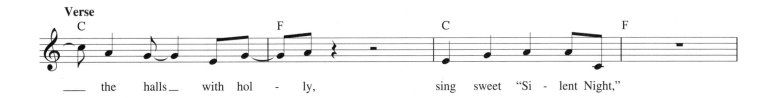

Verse

C   F   C   F

__ the halls __ with hol - ly, sing sweet "Si - lent Night,"

C   F   C   F

fill a tree __ with an - gel hair __ and pret - ty, pret - ty lights, __

C   F   C   F

go to sleep __ and wake __ up just be - fore __ day - light. __ And all __

Dm7

__ these things and more, __ ba - by, that's __ what Christ - (All these things and more, __ ba - by.)

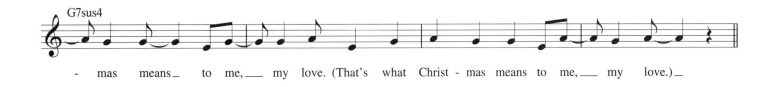

G7sus4

- mas means __ to me, __ my love. (That's what Christ - mas means to me, __ my love.) __

Outro

Repeat and fade

C   F   C   F

161

When Love Came Down

Written by Chris Eaton

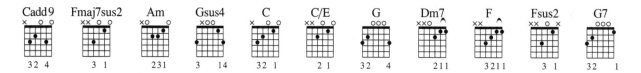

Strum Pattern: 3, 6
Pick Pattern: 4, 5

Intro   **Verse**

Moderately fast

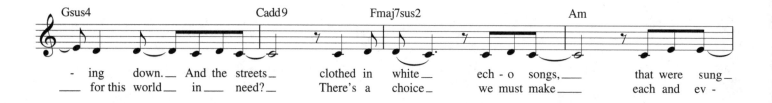

1. Christ-mas Eve, _____ two a. m.; _____ heav-y snow ___ is fall-
   ___ we can breathe; ___ but do we ___ real-ly care ___

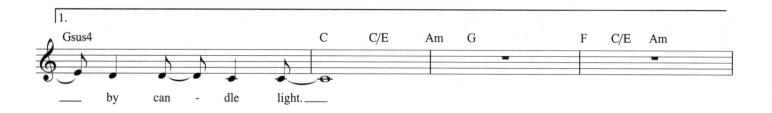

- ing down. ___ And the streets ___ clothed in white ___ ech-o songs, ___ that were sung ___
___ for this world ___ in ___ need? ___ There's a choice ___ we must make _____ each and ev-

___ by can-dle light. ___

___ 2. We're a-live ___ - 'ry day. ___ So, close your eyes ___ and share ___

___ the ___ dream; ___ let ev-'ry-one on earth ___ be-lieve. ___ The

© 1999 CLOUSEAU MUSIC and SGO MUSIC PUBLISHING, LTD. (PRS) /Administered by BUG MUSIC
All Rights Reserved   Used by Permission

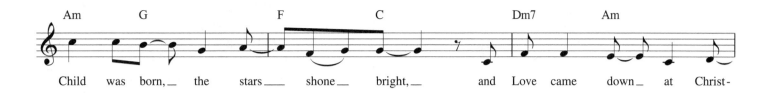

Child was born,__ the stars__ shone__ bright,__ and Love came down__ at Christ-

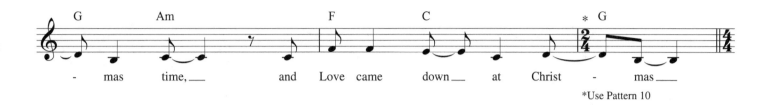

- mas time,__ and Love came down__ at Christ - mas__

*Use Pattern 10

Interlude

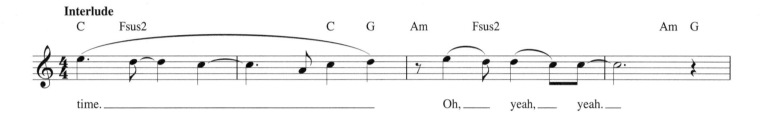

time._____ Oh,____ yeah,____ yeah.____

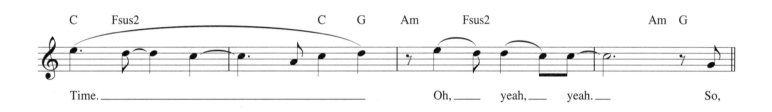

Time._____ Oh,____ yeah,____ yeah.____ So,

Bridge

Mer - ry Christ - mas ev - 'ry - one,__ and peace through-out__ the year.__

_____ The time has come__ to cel - e - brate,__ so

let your voic - es fill_____ the air.____ 3. Ev - 'ry - one,__

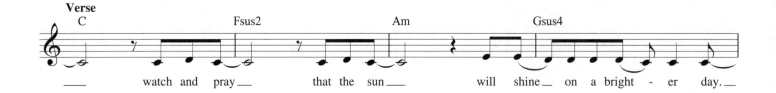

Verse

watch and pray ___ that the sun ___ will shine ___ on a bright - er day. ___

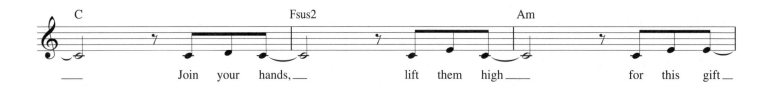

Join your hands, ___ lift them high ___ for this gift

___ of life. ___ When Love came down ___ at Christ - mas time. ___

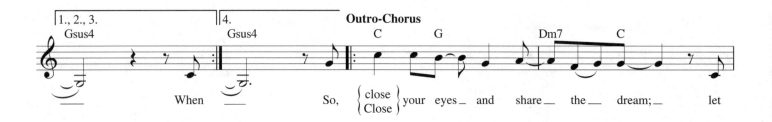

Outro-Chorus

When ___ When ___ So, {close / Close} your eyes ___ and share ___ the ___ dream; ___ let

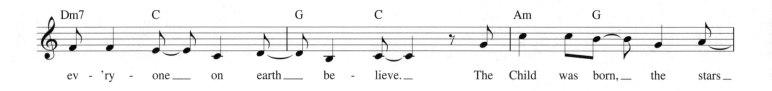

ev - 'ry - one ___ on earth ___ be - lieve. ___ The Child was born, ___ the stars ___

___ shone ___ bright, ___ and Love came down ___ at Christ - mas time. ___

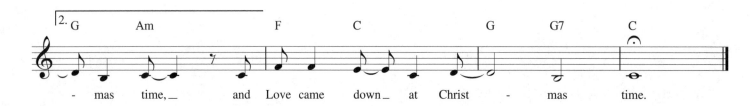

- mas time, ___ and Love came down ___ at Christ - mas time.

Where Are You Christmas?

from DR. SEUSS' HOW THE GRINCH STOLE CHRISTMAS
Words and Music by Will Jennings, James Horner and Mariah Carey

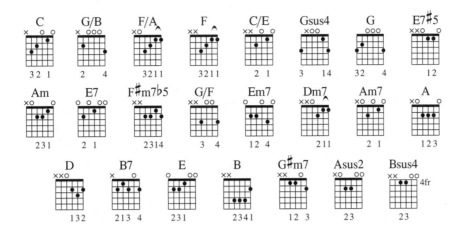

Strum Pattern: 2
Pick Pattern: 2, 4

Intro
Gently

1. Where are you,

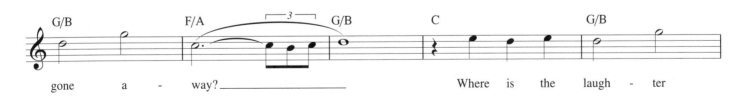

Christ - mas?   Why can't I find   you?   Why have you

gone a - way? _____   Where is the laugh - ter

you used to bring me?   Why can't I hear mu - sic play? _____

Copyright © 2000 BLUE SKY RIDER SONGS, UNIVERSAL MUSIC CORP., SONGS OF UNIVERSAL, INC.,
HORNER MUSIC, SONY/ATV SONGS LLC and RYE SONGS
All Rights for BLUE SKY RIDER SONGS Controlled and Administered by IRVING MUSIC, INC.
All Rights for SONY/ATV SONGS LLC and RYE SONGS Administered by SONY/ATV MUSIC PUBLISHING, 8 Music Square West, Nashville, TN 37203
All Rights Reserved   Used by Permission

Who Would Imagine a King

from the Touchstone Motion Picture THE PREACHER'S WIFE
Words and Music by Mervyn Warren and Hallerin Hilton Hill

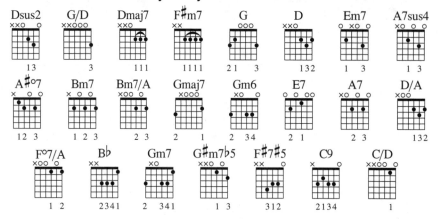

Strum Pattern: 8, 9
Pick Pattern: 7, 8

Verse
Moderately

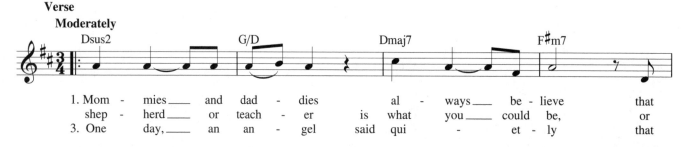

1. Mom - mies____ and dad - dies al - ways____ be - lieve that
   shep - herd____ or teach - er is what you ____ could be, or
3. One day,____ an an - gel said qui - et - ly that

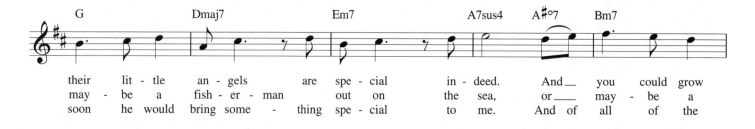

their lit - tle an - gels are spe - cial in - deed. And____ you could grow
may - be a fish - er - man out on the sea, or ____ may - be a
soon he would bring some - thing spe - cial to me. And of all of the

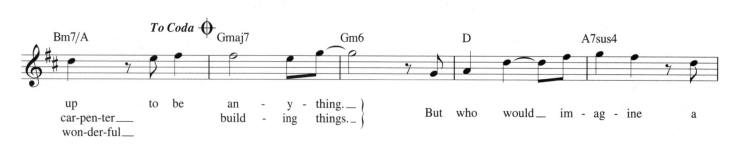

up to be an - y - thing.____)
car - pen - ter____ build - ing things.____)
won - der - ful____

But who would____ im - ag - ine a

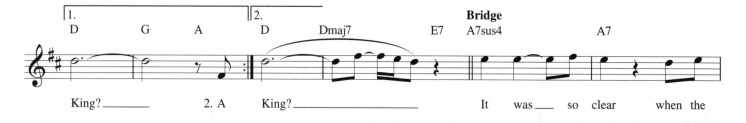

King?____ 2. A King?_____ It was____ so clear when the

© 1996 Buena Vista Music Company and Hallerin Hilton Hill Music (administered by MCS Music America, Inc.)
All Rights Reserved   Used by Permission

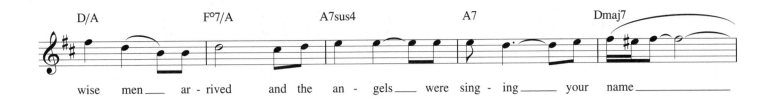

wise men ___ ar - rived   and the an - gels ___ were sing - ing ___ your name ___

___   that the world would be dif - f'rent 'cause you were ___ a - live.   That's why

D.C. al Coda

heav - en stood still ___   to pro - claim. ___

Coda

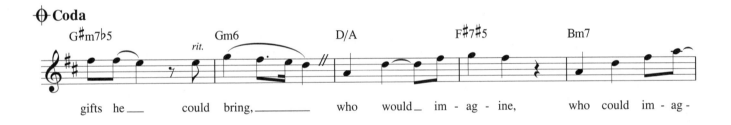

gifts he ___   could bring, ___   who would ___ im - ag - ine,   who could im - ag -

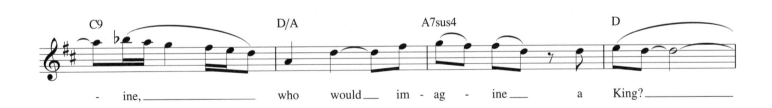

- ine, ___   who would ___ im - ag - ine ___ a   King? ___

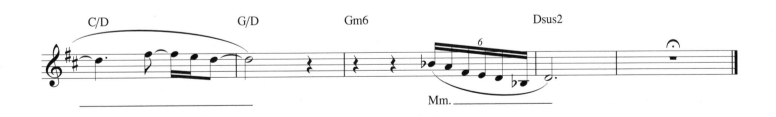

Mm. ___

Wonderful Christmastime

Words and Music by McCartney

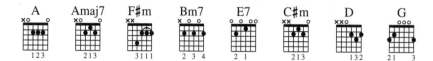

Strum Pattern: 2
Pick Pattern: 4

Verse

Brightly

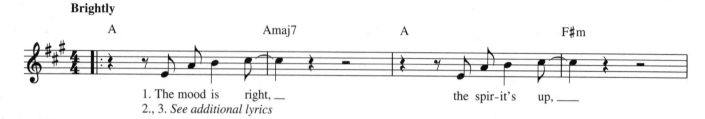

1. The mood is right, — the spir-it's up, —
2., 3. *See additional lyrics*

we're here to - night — and that's e - nough. —

Chorus

Sim - ply hav - ing a won - der - ful Christ - mas - time.

Sim - ply hav - ing a won - der - ful Christ - mas - time. time.

Bridge

The choir of chil - dren sing their song. (They prac - tised

To Coda ⊕

all year long.) Ding dong, ding dong. Ding dong, ding.

© 1979 MPL COMMUNICATIONS LTD.
Administered by MPL COMMUNICATIONS, INC.
All Rights Reserved

We're sim - ply hav - ing a won - der - ful Christ mas -

D.C. al Coda
(take 2nd ending)

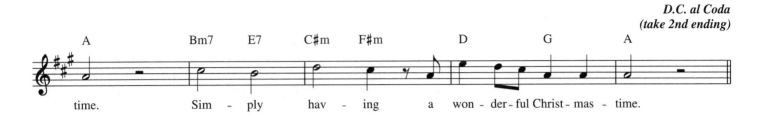

time. Sim - ply hav - ing a won - der - ful Christ - mas - time.

⊕ Coda

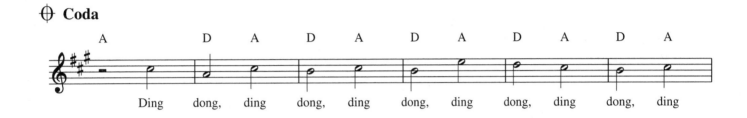

Ding dong, ding dong, ding dong, ding dong, ding dong, ding

dong, dong dong, dong, dong. The par - ty's on, ___ the spir-it's up, ___

___ we're here to - night ___ and that's e -nough. ___

Outro   *Repeat and fade*

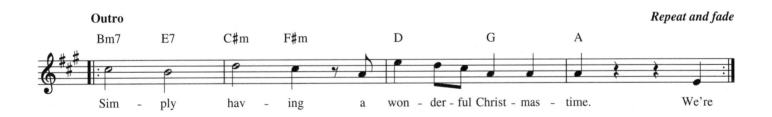

Sim - ply hav - ing a won - der - ful Christ - mas - time.   We're

Additional Lyrics

2. The party's on,
   The feeling's here
   That only comes
   This time of year.

3. The word is out
   About the town,
   To lift a glass.
   Oh, don't look down.

You Make It Feel Like Christmas

Words and Music by Neil Diamond

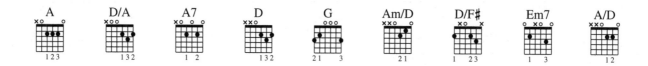

Strum Pattern: 4
Pick Pattern: 3

Intro

Moderately slow Rock

Co - zy we are, clos - er than far, sounds of for - ev - er still _

Verse

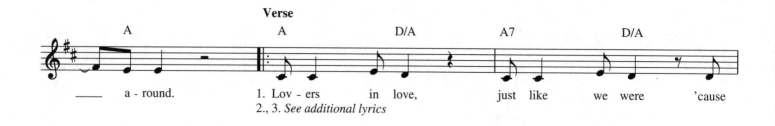

___ a - round. 1. Lov - ers in love, just like we were 'cause
2., 3. *See additional lyrics*

be - in' a - part's a lone - ly sound. And when peo - ple ask how __

we stay to - geth - er, I say you nev - er let ___ me down. __ { Yeah, 'Cause And }

© 1984 STONEBRIDGE MUSIC
All Rights Reserved

Chorus

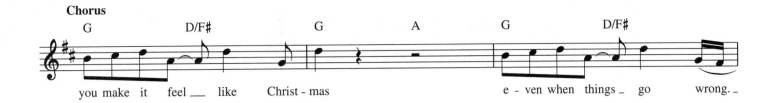

you make it feel ___ like Christ-mas   e - ven when things _ go   wrong. _

___   I hear the sound _ of   Christ-mas   in your song _

_   all   year   long.

That's how you know that it's true, ba - by.

3. Just   Yes, you know I do   babe,

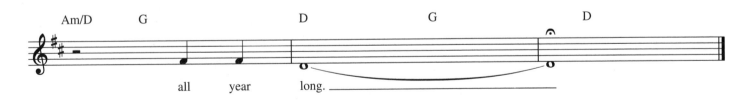

all   year   long. ___

Additional Lyrics

2. Look at the sun shining on me;
   Nowhere could be a better place.
   Lovers in love, yeah, that's what we'll be.
   When you're here with me, it's Christmas Day.

3. Just look at us now, part of it all.
   In spite of it all, we're still around.
   So wake up the kids, and put on some tea.
   Let's light up the tree; it's Christmas Day.

Why Christmas

Words and Music by Wanya Morris

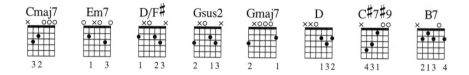

Strum Pattern: 6
Pick Pattern: 4

Verse
Slow R & B

1. Ev - 'ry day ___ at this ___ time of ___ year I won - der time ___ and time ___

___ a - gain ___ why are kids ___ suf - er - ing? ___

All ___ of ___ the tears ___ 'cause

be - ing caught ___ in the ___ cross - fi - re. ___ Some - bod -

- y tell ___ me ___ why. As ___ the joy - ous day ___

___ comes a - long, the eld - est feel ___ there's some - thing wrong. ___ He's

Copyright © 1993 by Squirt Shot Publishing and Ensign Music Corporation
International Copyright Secured   All Rights Reserved

look-in' for Mom___ but she's___ not there.___ Kids are look-ing for rein - deer in___

___ the air._____ She messed up a - gain._____ Why?___

𝄋 Chorus

___ My___ broth - er and___ my sis - ter, they ain't got___ no toys.___

___ What am I___ sup - posed___ to do___ when grow - ing up for me___ was-n't joy?___

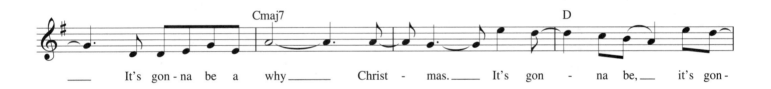

___ It's gon - na be a why_____ Christ - mas.___ It's gon - na be,___ it's gon-

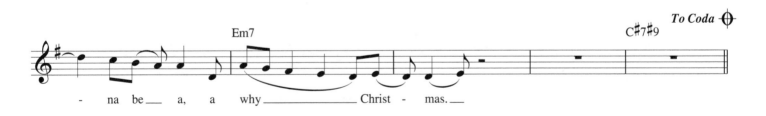

- na be___ a, a why_____ Christ - mas.___

Verse

2. No one was there___ but Grand - ma and her___ friends; the time of heart - ache___

set - ting___ in. There ain't noth - ing___ I___ can do_____ just

sit___ and feel___ pain run___ me through.___ I___ of - ten wished___

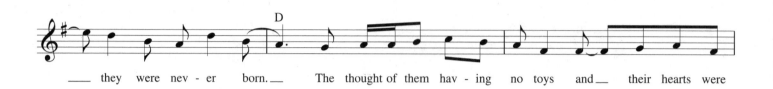

___ they were nev - er born.___ The thought of them hav - ing no toys and___ their hearts were

torn.___ I was young___ and I cried_____ as well,_____ oh,___ yeah.

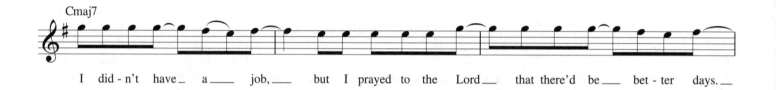

I did-n't have___ a___ job,___ but I prayed to the Lord___ that there'd be___ bet - ter days.___

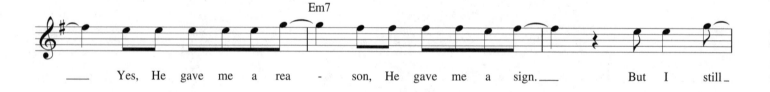

___ Yes, He gave me a rea - son, He gave me a sign.___ But I still_

___ think to___ that___ day___ when she messed up a - gain,___ she messed

up a - gain___ and I won - der_____ why?_____

♦ Coda

Bro - ther and___ my, bro - ther and___ my, bro - ther and___ my sis - ter.

176